Readings in

VISUALLY HANDICAPPED EDUCATION

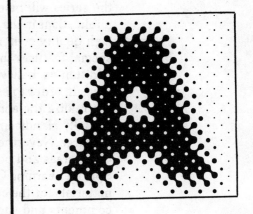

Special Learning Corporation

42 Boston Post Rd. Guilford, Connecticut 06437

SPECIAL LEARNING CORPORATION

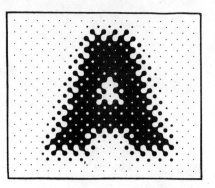

Publisher's Message:

The Special Education Series is the first comprehensive series designed for special education courses of study. It is also the first series to offer such a wide variety of high quality books. In addition, the series will be expanded and up-dated each year. No other publications in the area of special education can equal this. We stress high quality content, a superb advisory and consulting group, and special features that help in understanding the course of study. In addition we believe we must also publish in very small enrollment areas in order to establish the credibility and strength of our series. We realize the enrollments in courses of study such as Autism, Visually Handicapped Education, or Diagnosis and Placement are not large. Nevertheless, we believe there is a need for course books in these areas and books that are kept up-to-date on an annual basis! Special Learning Corporation's goal is to publish the highest quality materials for the college and university courses of study. With your comments and support we will continue to do this.

John P. Quirk

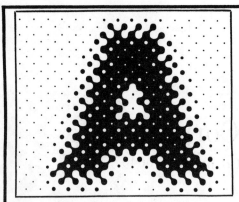

©1978 by Special Learning Corporation, Guilford, Connecticut 06437

First Edition

3 4 5

ISBN No.   0-89568-010-6

CONTENTS

3. Educational and Vocational Support Systems

4. Emerging Trends in Rehabilitative Services

Focus II   96

TOPIC MATRIX

Readings in Visually Handicapped education provides the college student in special education an overview of the nature, needs and educational techniques in teaching the visually handicapped.

COURSE OUTLINE:

Foundations of the Education of the Visually Handicapped Child

I. The history of education of the visually handicapped
II. Psychology and social adjustment of the visually impaired
III. Learning problems of the visually impaired
IV. The visually impaired in society today

Readings in Visually Handicapped

I. Education of the Visually Handicapped
II. Etiology of Visual Impairment
III. Educational and Vocational Support Systems
IV. Emerging Trends in Rehabilitative Services

Related Special Learning Corporation Readers

I. Readings in Special Education
II. Readings in Mainstreaming
III. Readings in Diagnosis and Placement
IV. Readings in Psychology of Exceptional Children

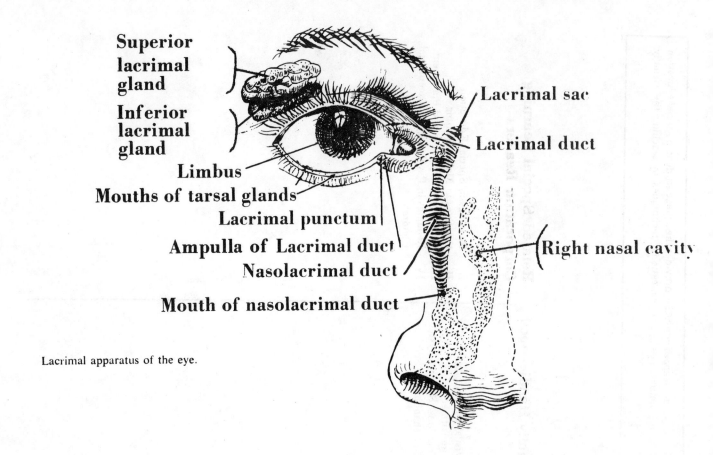

Superior
lacrimal
gland

Inferior
lacrimal
gland

Lacrimal sac

Lacrimal duct

Limbus

Mouths of tarsal glands

Lacrimal punctum

Ampulla of Lacrimal duct

Nasolacrimal duct

Mouth of nasolacrimal duct

Right nasal cavity

Lacrimal apparatus of the eye.

Sideview cross section of the right eye.

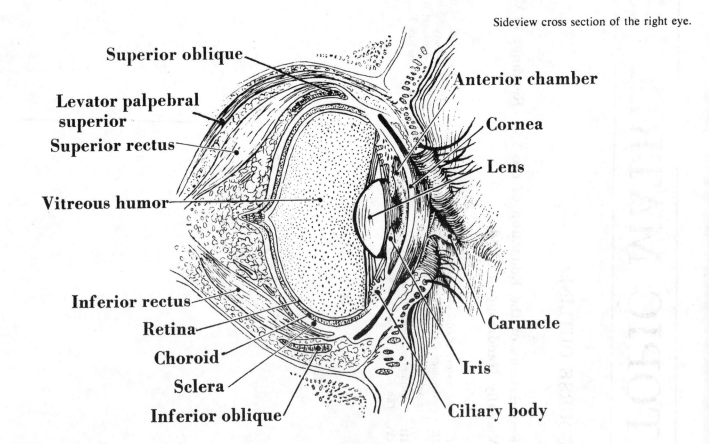

Superior oblique

Levator palpebral
superior

Superior rectus

Vitreous humor

Inferior rectus

Retina

Choroid

Sclera

Inferior oblique

Anterior chamber

Cornea

Lens

Caruncle

Iris

Ciliary body

GLOSSARY OF TERMS

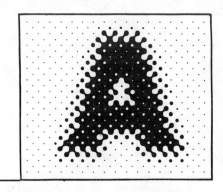

after-image Visual impression which remains after a stimulus is removed.

asthenopia Dimness of vision without any apparent cause.

amblyopia ex anopsia Ablyopia acquired through lack of use of the eye.

astigmatism Defective curvature of the refractive surfaces of the eye as a result of which light rays are not sharply focused on the retina for either near or distance.

cataract A condition in which the crystalline lens of the eye becomes opaque for consequent loss of visual acuity.

contact or corneal lenses Lenses so constructed that they fit directly on the eyeball; used for the correction of vision in cases having a cone-shaped cornea and for cosmetic reasons. Corneal lenses are also used after cataract (lens) extraction to replace the lens removed from the eye because they provide less distortion and image size difference from the other eye than spectacles would.

corneal graft Operation to restore vision by replacing a section of opaque cornea with transparent cornea.

esophoria Latent tendency of the eye to turn inward
esotropia An observable turning in of one eye (convergent strabismus or crossed eye).

focus Point to which rays are converted after passing through a lens; focal distance is the distance rays travel after refraction before focus is reached.

glaucoma Disease of the eye marked by a mechanical increase in the intraocular pressure causing organic changes in the optic nerve and defects in the visual field.

herpes simplex Cold sores on cornea.

iris Colored, circular membrane suspended behind the cornea immediately in front of the lens, which regulates the amount of light entering the eye chamber by changing the size of the pupil.

microphthalmia Abnormal smallness of the eyes.

myopia A refractive error in which rays of light come to a focus in front of the retina as a result of eyeball being to long from front to back, or having excessive curvature of cornea or lens.

optician Grinds lenses, fits them into frames, and adjusts frames to the wearer.

opthalmologist A physician who specializes in diagnosis and treatment of defects and diseases of the eye.

optometrist A person who examines, measures, and treats certain eye defects by methods requiring no physician's license.

presbyopia Decreased elasticity in the eyeball causing some loss of accomodation, and usually seen in older persons.

refraction The bending or deviation of rays of light in passing obliquely from one medium to another of different density; the determination of the refractive errors of the eye and their correction by prescription glasses.

sphincter muscle Muscle which contracts to make the pupil smaller.

strabismus Manifest deviation of the eyes so that they are not simultaneously directed to the same object; see heterotrophia.

stye Acute inflammation of a sabaceous gland in the margin of the eyelid due to infection.

tonometer Instrument used in measuring tension or pressure in order to check for glaucoma.

trachoma Chronic contagious conjunctivitis producing loss of vision.

vision The ability to see and interpret what is seen.

visual acuity Sharpness of vision, the ability of the eye to distinguish detail.

PREFACE

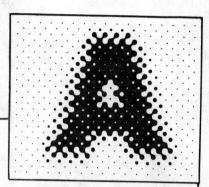

The eyes have been called the most complete view of a man's inner being. The eyes can reveal to others stronger feeling than can verbal expression. Judgements are often formed by looking at a person's eyes . . . Historically, seeing has been considered one of the five most important senses.

The blind have had to cultivate other senses, like hearing or a keen sense of smell to compensate for what they might otherwise miss. Tactile sense comes through their fingers in the form of braille as a substitute for the printed word. When the simple mechanisms of seeing are impaired or non-existant, we classify these children as partially-seeing—approximately four out of every 2,000 children require some variation of special education as a result of their degree of visual difficulty. One of every 2,000 children is blind, with varying numbers in different countries around the world. Over 330 of each 100,000 people in the world experience blindness.

Those who see partially, may be classified within three main categories—the first being those who experience an impairment in the acuity of vision. The second type experience non-communicable disease of the eye such as a myopic condition, and the third type experiences various cases of chronic eye weakness, with possible injury to the eye which will need specially designed close attention.

For those who experience the extremes of blindness, pride remains their most valued and important asset. Various phases of blindness have been discovered, including perfected methods of teaching of the psychology and physiology of the blind, with the establishment of schools and classes, and special legal provisions for their care in society.

Readings in Visually Handicapped Education offers a broad over-view of the physiology of the anatomy of vision, the partially-seeing, and of the blind. It is one of our series of readers which delves into the sensory disorders and defects which have challenged mankind through the ages and which we strive to perfect through the latest information for our education and betterment in this field.

A Blind Person Is Always Alone

by Tsugu Kagimoto (ninth-grade boy)

O Lord, Please Listen to Me

by Keiko Kawai (eighth-grade girl)

Education of the Visually Handicapped

Pertinent factors indicate that 20 percent of all children have some form or degree of visual defect or disease which is correctable in a majority of cases. For greater visual handicaps there are four in every 2,000 who require some type of special education sightsaving class.

For the partially-seeing educational alternatives lie with schools for the blind in a residential setting, special day schools, special segregated classes in a large school system, itinerant teacher plans, and regular classroom settings. Classrooms must be especially designed to hold smaller numbers of students in various grades within one room. Nonreflective surfaces and lack of direct outside light must be held to a minimum of 85 percent reflectance for proper illumination and comfort.

Teaching aids should include large-type books in 18 point to 24 point size. Special typewriters and desks are also essential for effective education. Teachers are specially trained in anatomy, physiology and hygiene of the eye and vision. They must also meet requirements in mental hygiene, arts and crafts, and typewriting skills.

For those who experience the grave extremes of blindness, education in the functional definition is quite another matter. A person is termed "blind" in the educational sense if he cannot learn print, but requires instruction in braille. Educational programs include state residential schools, special classes within the public school system, and itinerant teacher plans where blind pupils may remain in their natural social setting. Early on, education of the blind was a very difficult process. However, with the progress of today's technology, the blind can now utilize braille to acquire reading and writing skills, Talking Books, record players, relief maps, arithmetic boards, and the latest in computer designed aids.

Teachers for the blind undertake extensive specialized training in anatomy and physiology of the eye, remedial and preventive measures, operation of talking books and other equipment, the correct use of special typewriters, and most importantly, a complete knowledge of how one reads and writes braille for teaching purposes.

Whether a person is visually handicapped or blind the psychology of learning and human endeavor match those who experience normal patterns of life. We must always consider that the visually handicapped person is a human being first, with physical, emotional, intellectual, and social attributes which combine to form a life of happiness and success with their acquisition of knowledge gained through education.

HELEN KELLER

The story of Helen Keller is the story of a normal child who, at the age of 18 months, was suddenly shut off from the world but who, against overwhelming odds, waged a slow, hard, but successful battle to re-enter that same world. The near-savage little deaf and blind mute grew into a highly intelligent and sensitive woman who wrote, spoke, and labored incessantly for the betterment of others. So powerful a symbol of triumph over adversity did she become that she has a definite place in the history of our time and of times to come.

Helen Adams Keller was born, physically whole and healthy, in Tuscumbia, Alabama on June 27, 1880 in a white frame cottage called "Ivy Green." On her father's side she was descended from Alexander Spottswood, a colonial governor of Virginia, and connected with the Lees and other Southern families. On her mother's side, she was related to a number of prominent New England families, including the Hales, the Everetts, and the Adams. Her father, Captain Arthur Keller, was the editor of a newspaper, the *North Tuscumbia Alabaman.* Captain Keller also had a strong interest in public life and was an influential figure in his own community. In 1885, under the Cleveland administration, he was appointed Marshal of North Alabama.

The illness that struck the infant Helen Keller and left her deaf, blind, and mute was diagnosed as brain fever at the time; perhaps it was scarlet fever. Popular belief had it that the disease left its victim an idiot. And as Helen Keller grew from infancy into childhood, wild, unruly, and with little real understanding of the world around her, this belief was seemingly confirmed.

Helen Keller's real life began on a March day in 1887 when she was a few months short of seven years old. On that day, which Miss Keller was always to call "The most important day I can remember in my life," Anne Mansfield Sullivan came to Tuscumbia to be her teacher. Miss Sullivan, a 20-year-old graduate of the Perkins School for the Blind who had regained useful sight through a series of operations, had come to the Kellers through the sympathetic interest of Alexander Graham Bell. From that fateful day, the two—teacher and pupil—were inseparable until the death of the former in 1936.

How Miss Sullivan turned the near-savage child into a responsible human being and succeeded in awakening her marvelous mind is familiar to millions, most notably through William Gibson's play and film, *The Miracle Worker,* and through Miss Keller's own autobiography of her early years, *The Story of My Life.*

Miss Sullivan began her task with a doll the children at Perkins had made for her to take to Helen. By spelling "d-o-l-l" into the child's hand, she hoped to teach her to connect objects with letters. Helen quickly learned to make the letters correctly, but did not know that she was spelling a word, or that words existed. In the days that followed she learned to spell a great many more words in this uncomprehending way.

One day she and "Teacher"—as Helen always called her—were standing beside the outdoor pump while

Helen Keller with one of her earliest mentors, Alexander Graham Bell.

Miss Keller and Annie Sullivan.

someone was drawing water. Miss Sullivan put Helen's hand under the spout. As the cool water gushed over one hand, she spelled into the other the word "w-a-t-e-r" first slowly, then rapidly. Suddenly, the signals had meaning in Helen's mind. She knew that "water" meant the wonderful cool something flowing over her hand. Quickly, she stopped and touched the earth and demanded its letter name and by nightfall she had learned 30 words.

Thus began Helen Keller's education. She proceeded quickly to mastering the alphabet, both manual and in raised print for the blind, and gained facility in reading and writing. In 1890, when she was just 10, she expressed a desire to learn how to speak. Somehow she had found out that a little deaf-blind girl in Norway had acquired that ability. Miss Sarah Fuller of the Horace Mann School was her first speech teacher.

Even when she was a little girl, Helen Keller said, "Someday I shall go to college." And go to college she did. In 1898 she entered the Cambridge School for Young Ladies to prepare for Radcliffe College. She entered Radcliffe in the fall of 1900 and received her bachelor of arts degree *cum laude* in 1904. Throughout these years and until her own death in 1936, Anne Sullivan was always by Helen's side, laboriously spelling book after book and lecture after lecture, into her pupil's hand.

Helen Keller's formal schooling ended when she received her B.A. degree. But throughout her life she continued to study and keep informed on all matters of importance to modern man. In recognition of her wide knowledge and many scholastic achievements, she received honorary doctoral degrees from Temple University and Harvard University and from the Universities of Glasgow, Scotland; Berlin, Germany; Delhi, India; and Witwaterstrand, Johannesburg, South Africa. She was also an Honorary Fellow of the Educational Institute of Scotland.

Anne Sullivan's marriage, in 1905, to John Macy, an eminent critic and prominent socialist, caused no change in the teacher-pupil relationship.

Helen went to live with the Macys and both husband and wife gave unstintingly of their time to help her with her studies and other activities.

While still a student at Radcliffe, Helen Keller began the writing career that was to continue on and off for 50 years. In 1902, *The Story of My Life,* which had first appeared in serial form in the *Ladies Home Journal,* appeared in book form. This was always to be the most popular of her works and today it is available in more than 50 languages including Marathi, Pushtu, Tagalog, and Vedu. It is also available in several paperback editions in this country.

Miss Keller's other published works include *Optimism,* an essay; *The World I Live In; The Song of the Stone Wall; Out of the Dark; My Religion; Midstream —My Later Life; Peace at Eventide; Helen Keller in Scotland; Helen Keller's Journal; Let Us Have Faith; Teacher, Annie Sullivan Macy;* and *The Open Door.*

In addition, she was a frequent contributor to magazines and newspapers, writing most frequently on blindness, deafness, socialism, social issues, and women's rights. She used a braille typewriter to prepare her manuscripts and then copied them on a regular typewriter.

During her lifetime, Helen Keller received awards of great distinction too numerous to recount fully here. An entire room, called the Helen Keller Room, is devoted to their display at the American Foundation for the Blind in New York City. These awards include Brazil's Order of the Southern Cross; Japan's Sacred Treasure; the Philippines' Golden Heart; Lebanon's Gold Medal of Merit; and her own country's highest civilian honor, the Presidential Medal of Freedom. Most of these awards were bestowed upon her in recognition of the stimulation her example and presence gave to work for the blind in those countries. In 1952 during the Louis Braille Centennial Commemoration, Miss Keller was made a Chevalier of the French Legion of Honor at a ceremony in the Sorbonne.

On the 50th anniversary of her

graduation, Radcliffe College granted her its Alumnae Achievement Award. Her Alma Mater also showed its pride in her by dedicating the Helen Keller Garden in her honor, and by naming a fountain in the garden for Anne Sullivan Macy.

Miss Keller also received the Americas Award for Inter-American Unity, the Gold Medal Award from the National Institute of Social Sciences, the National Humanitarian Award from Variety Clubs International, and many others. She held honorary memberships in scientific societies and philanthropic organizations throughout the world.

Yet another honor came to Helen Keller in 1954 when her birthplace, "Ivy Green," in Tuscumbia, was made a permanent shrine. It was dedicated on May 7, 1954 with officials of the American Foundation for the Blind, American Foundation for Overseas Blind, and many other agencies and organizations present. In conjunction with this event, the premiere of Miss Keller's film biography, *The Unconquered,* produced by Nancy Hamilton and narrated by Katharine Cornell, was held in the nearby city of Birmingham. The film was later renamed *Helen Keller in Her Story* and in 1955 won an "Oscar"—the Academy of Motion Picture Arts and Sciences award as the best feature-length documentary film of the year.

Miss Keller was indirectly responsible for two other "Oscars" a few years later when Anne Bancroft and Patty Duke won them for their portrayals of Anne Sullivan and Helen Keller in the film version of *The Miracle Worker.*

More rewarding to her than the many honors she received, were the acquaintances and friendships Helen Keller made with most of the leading personalities of her time. There were few world figures, from Grover Cleveland to Charlie Chaplin, to Nehru to John F. Kennedy, that she did not meet. And many, among them Katharine Cornell, Van Wyck Brooks, Alexander Graham Bell, Jo Davidson, she counted as friends. Two friends from her early youth, Mark Twain and William James, expressed beautifully what most of her

1. AN OVERVIEW

friends felt about her. Mark Twain said, "The two most interesting characters of the 19th century are Napoleon and

Horseback riding, along with swimming and walking, were Miss Keller's favorite physical activities.

Helen Keller." William James wrote, "But whatever you were or are, you're a blessing!"

As broad and wide-ranging as her interests were, Helen Keller never lost sight of the needs of her fellow blind and deaf-blind. From her youth, she was always willing to help them by appearing before legislatures, giving lectures, writing articles, and above all, by her own example of what a severely handicapped person could accomplish. When the American Foundation for the Blind, the national clearing house for information on blindness, was established in 1921, she at last had an effective national outlet for her efforts. From 1924 until her death she was a member of the Foundation staff, serving as counselor on national and international relations. It was also in 1924 that Miss Keller began her campaign to raise the "Helen Keller Endowment Fund" for the Foundation. Until her retirement from public life, she was tireless in her efforts to make the Fund adequate for the Foundation's needs.

Of all her contributions to the Foundation, Miss Keller was perhaps most proud of her assistance in the formation in 1946 of its special

service for deaf-blind persons. She was, of course, deeply concerned for this group of people and was always searching for ways to help those "less fortunate than myself."

Helen Keller was as interested in the welfare of blind persons in other countries as she was for those in her own country; conditions in the underdeveloped and war-ravaged nations were of particular concern. Her active participation in this area of work for the blind began as early as 1915 when the Permanent Blind Relief War Fund, later called the American Braille Press, was founded. She was a member of its first board of directors.

When the American Braille Press became the American Foundation for Overseas Blind (a sister organization to the American Foundation for the Blind) in 1946, Miss Keller was appointed counselor on international relations. It was then that she began the globe-circling tours on behalf of the blind for which she was so well known during her later years. During seven trips between 1946 and 1957 she visited 35 countries on five continents. In 1955, when she was 75 years old, she embarked on one of her longest and most grueling journeys, a 40,000-mile, five-month tour through Asia. Wherever she traveled, she brought new courage to millions of blind people, and many of the efforts to improve conditions among the blind abroad can be traced directly to her visits.

In May 1959, the American Foundation for Overseas Blind started the Helen Keller World Crusade for the Blind in a ceremony held at the United Nations in New York City. Miss Keller's long-time close friend, Katharine Cornell, was named chairman. At the time, Miss Keller was almost 80 years old and realized that she could no longer participate as actively in the foundation's work as she once had. She looked to the Crusade to carry on and expand her work overseas and keep alive the hope inspired in the countries she had visited.

In 1960, on the occasion of her 80th birthday, the American Foundation for Overseas Blind established the Helen

Keller International Award for Distinguished Service to the Blind, to be presented periodically to individuals who have made outstanding contributions to work for the blind at the world level or in countries other than the United States. This award, called "The Spirit of Helen Keller," is a bronze figure symbolic of Miss Keller's indomitable spirit.

During her lifetime, Helen Keller lived in many different places—Tuscumbia, Alabama; Cambridge and Wrentham, Massachusetts; Forest Hills, New York, but perhaps her favorite residence was her last, the house in Westport, Connecticut she called Arcan Ridge. She moved to this white frame house surrounded by mementos of her rich and busy life after her beloved "Teacher's" death in 1936. And it was Arcan Ridge she called home for the rest of her life. "Teacher's" death, although it left her with a heavy heart, did not leave Helen alone. Polly Thomson, a Scots woman who joined the Keller household in 1914, assumed the task of assisting Helen with her work. After Miss Thomson's death in 1960, various companions assisted Miss Keller.

Helen Keller made her last major public appearance in 1961 at a Washington, D.C. Lions Club Meeting. At that meeting she received the Lions Humanitarian Award for her lifetime of service to humanity and for providing the inspiration for the adoption by Lions International of their sight conservation and aid to the blind programs. During that visit to Washington, she also called on President Kennedy at the White House. After that White House visit, a reporter asked her how many of our presidents she had met. She replied that she did not know how many, but that she had met all of them since Grover Cleveland!

After 1961, Helen Keller lived quietly at Arcan Ridge. She saw her family, close friends, and associates from the American Foundation for the Blind and the American Foundation for Overseas Blind, and spent much time reading. Her favorite books were the Bible and volumes of poetry and philosophy.

Despite her retirement from public

life, Helen Keller was not forgotten. In 1964 she received the previously mentioned Presidential Medal of Freedom. In 1965, she was one of 20 elected to the Women's Hall of Fame at the New York World's Fair. Miss Keller and Eleanor Roosevelt received the most votes among the 100 nominees.

Helen Keller died on June 1, 1968 at Arcan Ridge, a few weeks short of her 88th birthday. She was buried next to her beloved companions, Anne Sullivan Macy and Polly Thomson, in the St. Joseph's Chapel of Washington Cathedral. The burial was preceded by a public memorial service in the Cathedral attended by government officials, prominent persons from all walks of life, delegations from most of the organizations for the blind and the deaf, friends and family.

"Teacher" and Miss Keller visit Charlie Chaplin on a Hollywood movie set.

Louis Braille

Everyone knows that braille is the touch system of reading and writing used by blind people throughout the world. It has done for them what the printed word has done for the sighted—and perhaps more, since blind people need a greater amount of description to compensate for lack of visual experience. It has given them a means of expressing the words of English and other languages in written form. It has given them the freedom that comes with the ability to communicate. For the deaf-blind braille has been a godsend.

What not everyone may know is that braille writing got its name from its inventor, Louis Braille, who is today greatly honored for his achievement.

But his story is that of a man who was to achieve recognition slowly. For the greater part of his own lifetime, the braille system was known to members of the school where Louis Braille was educated and later taught, but to few outsiders. Those who had an interest in the welfare of blind people were slow to change the unsatisfactory methods used to educate people who could not see well enough to read ordinary books.

It was only towards the end of his life that use of Braille's writing began to spread. Even so, the significance of his accomplishment remained unacknowledged by the public.

As early as 1878, a group in favor of making braille the official international system of writing for blind people met in Paris. In 1918 the United States recognized the superiority of braille over other methods when the American Association of Instructors of the Blind and the American Association of Workers for the Blind approved a revised form of braille known as Revised Braille Grade One and One Half; but it was not until 1932 that agreement was reached on a standardized Engish braille code. This is called Standard English Braille Grade Two. Today the revised system simply known as English Braille has put an end to competing variations on the touch writing system and made possible the exchange of English-language published materials, like books, pamphlets, and magazines, which can be put into braille in various English-speaking countries, thus benefitting all braille readers.

In 1952, a century after his death, Braille's remains were taken from their resting place in his native village of Coupvray for burial in the Pantheon, the greatest honor France can bestow upon its citizens. While representatives from forty nations paid their respects, Louis Braille at last took his place among the great men of France.

To realize his importance, it is first necessary to explain briefly the braille system—what it is and how it is used. It is then that the man and his genius can be explained.

braille is a system of touch reading and writing in which raised dots represent the letters of the alphabet. An arrangement of six dots comprise what is referred to as the braille cell. For the purpose of identification, the dots have been numbered downward, 1-2-3 on the left and 4-5-6 on the right.

```
1 • • 4
2 • • 5
3 • • 6
```

By arranging the dots in various combinations, 63 different patterns are possible. It is some of these dot patterns which represent the letters and punctuation marks. When braille was originally invented, each dot pattern stood for a specific letter and words were spelled out in the traditional manner. Today, although braille can still be used in this way, several forms of contractions have been developed. (For example, the letter "b," when it is not preceded or followed by another letter or a contraction, represents the word "but.") Only the contractions of English Braille are used when producing braille editions of published materials. The use of Grade Three Braille, a highly contracted system, is a matter of individual choice. It may be used when taking notes at a lecture, a conference, or in other similar situations. Because Grade Three Braille editions of published materials were found to be extremely difficult to read, this system has been rejected by the great majority of braille readers.

Braille is read by moving the hand or hands from left to right along each line. Although most readers read predominantly with one hand, both hands are usually involved in the reading process, and there are two-handed readers who can make strong use of the second hand. Reading is generally done with the index finger, but the middle and ring fingers can also be used. The average reading speed is about 104 words per minute, but some people can read up to 125 words per minute with one hand and 250 words per minute with both hands.

before the development of braille writing by Louis Braille in 1824 blind people had no satisfactory means of written communication. Learning through oral teaching was difficult and limited, and the majority of blind people received little or no education. If their families were wealthy, they would probably be protected and eventually live on a pension; but blind children of poor families might even be turned out into the streets. There they could only become beggars or do the crudest menial tasks. Few blind people, rich or poor, were able to lead productive lives.

It was Louis Braille who, blinded by an accident in his early childhood, through his own misfortune was able to bring hope to other blind people.

Louis Braille was born January 4 in the year 1809 in the little French village of Coupvray, about 28 miles from Paris. His father, Simon René Braille, was the local harness-maker, a master craftsman who was able to support his family in a simple but comfortable manner. His mother, Monique Baron, was a farm girl who had come from a nearby village to wed Louis' father in 1792, 17 years before the child's birth. Little Louis was the youngest by 12 years of four children. It was said he would be the comfort of his parents' old age.

The little stone house in which the Braille family lived is still standing today and is now a museum which is open to the public. The street is now named Louis Braille Street.

Louis Braille, with his light hair and blue eyes, was an alert and happy baby. One day when he was only three years old, he was at play in his father's workshop. Picking up one of the sharp tools—it may have been an awl—he tried to imitate his father's work. Suddenly the tool slipped and went into his eye.

Although his frightened parents did all they could, hygiene was not what it is today, and the infection, which may have begun as conjunctivitis, spread. Because the child did not know better and rubbed his eyes with his hands, the eye which had not been injured became infected. Louis Braille became completely blind.

Aware of the miserable kind of life which awaited most blind people, Simon René Braille and his wife wished to help their son to the best of their abilities. However, they saw few, if any, possibilities open to them. Since Louis was an intelligent and curious child, his parents had good cause to worry about his future.

It was fortunate that first the parish priest, the Abbé Jacques Palluy, and then the village school teacher, Antoine Becheret, recognized Louis' superior learning abilities.

1. AN OVERVIEW

At the request of the priest, seven-year-old Louis was allowed to sit in the schoolroom. It was not expected that he would be able to keep up with the other pupils. Then he began to recite what he had learned. With the encouragement of his teacher, the boy was able to reach the head of his class.

When Louis Braille was ten years old, he succeeded in obtaining a scholarship to the Royal Institution for Blind Youth in Paris. When he arrived, he was the youngest student there. There the pupils were taught primarily by repeating the lessons given to them by their professors and by older students. In addition, there were a few books printed using a system developed by Valentin Haüy, founder of the school, in which embossed letters took the place of inkprint. This method was not very efficient, but it was the best that was available at the time.

Louis Braille was a good student. He enjoyed his courses, studied hard, and also was able to become first a pianist and later, a talented organ player. The teachers were strict and life at the Institution lacked many of the comforts of home, but Louis was anxious to learn and so, although he probably missed the fresh air and sunshine of the country, he rapidly entered into his new life. Along with his formal studies, Louis was becoming more and more interested in the idea of an alphabet for the blind.

The first person to invent a special form of touch writing that did not employ the standard letters of the alphabet was an artillery captain in the army of Louis XVIII, Charles Barbier de la Serre. Barbier had originally developed a system of "night writing" to be used by the soldiers on night maneuvers. He adapted this system into writing to be used by the blind, renaming his method Sonography.

The system consisted of raised dots and dashes on cardboard. However, words were spelled phonetically and, since it employed a 12-dot cell (which Louis Braille was later to cut in half), it took many dots to make up a single word. Barbier's method was complicated and diffcult to use. In spite of its drawbacks, however, this new system was to serve as a foundation for the braille method.

The then head of the Institution for Blind Youth, Dr. Pignier, had, like his recent predecessor, discussed the system with Barbier himself when the latter tried to have his method officially adopted by the Institution. Pignier approached the new method cautiously, promising only that he would inform the students and teachers. A meeting was held and the system met with an enthusiastic response. It was decided that it be adopted as an auxiliary teaching method.

Louis Braille was delighted. He soon began using his free time to learn Sonography. He and a friend would practice reading and embossing the dots themselves with the aid of a stylus and special sliding rule device. The more Louis learned, however, the more the faults of this method became apparent to him. In a short time he found himself making changes in the system.

When these changes were reported to Charles Barbier by Dr. Pignier, the inventor himself came to the school to discuss his system with Louis Braille. He was surprised to find himself face to face with a frail schoolboy. Although Barbier did agree with some of Braille's suggestions, he did not like having his system challenged by a mere youth. He insisted that his main concepts remain unchanged.

In a way Barbier's stubborness was a good thing. As a result of his argument with Braille, Louis realized that it would be best to turn his attention to a new system that would eliminate completely the problems of Sonography. Devoting himself to this fresh approach, he even began to stay awake nights working out his new ideas. When summer vacation came, he took his stylus and heavy paper home with him and continued his efforts. When the time came to return to the Institution, his work was finished. About three years had passed from the time he had first begun to experiment with the idea of creating an alphabet for blind people. Thus in 1824, at the age of fifteen, Louis Braille invented the system of writing which was to bear his name.

Having reached his goal, having so revolutionized the concept of touch reading and writing for blind people, Louis Braille did not stop his research. While still a student, as was the custom for older pupils at the Institution, he began teaching the younger students. He also took courses at the College de France and studied the organ. At the same time, he adapted his system of dot writing to include musical notation. In 1827 parts of the *Grammar of Grammars* had been translated into his system. By 1829, after his work with writing notes, the first edition of the *Method of Writing Words, Music and Plain Songs by Means of Dots, for Use by the Blind and Arranged for Them* was brought out.

Louis Braille had officially become an apprentice teacher in 1828, instructing pupils in mathematics, grammar, and geography. Of Braille as a teacher, Coltat, one of his students, later wrote in his *Historical Note on Louis Braille,* "He carried out his duties with so much charm and wisdom that the obligation of attending class was transformed into a real pleasure for his pupils.

They competed not only to equal and surpass each other, but also in a touching and constant effort to please a teacher whom they admired as a superior and liked as a wise and well-informed friend, ready with sound advice."

As an apprentice, however, he was treated as if he were merely an older pupil. The strict rules of the Institution still had to be obeyed. He could not even leave the school grounds without permission. He must have been very happy when, five years later, he was promoted to regular teacher.

Louis Braille continued to live at the Institution, although he did have more of an outside social life, partially because Dr. Pignier took an interest in the lives of his young teachers and encouraged them to go places with him. At parties Braille was often asked to play the piano. He may have enjoyed these evenings out, but it is likely that he had mixed feelings about socializing, since a blind person was likely to be regarded with pity. Also, his health was beginning to fail and he tired easily.

Then, when he was 26, Louis Braille discovered that he had contracted tuberculosis. In those days there was no cure for this disease. Rest was prescribed. At best, treatment could only prolong the patient's life.

In spite of the need to reduce his work load for the sake of his health, he began to devote himself to developing a means of written communication between the blind and the sighted. He realized that because few sighted persons would be willing to learn his dot writing, it would be necessary for blind people to learn to write the regular alphabet. Today, of course, the easiest thing for a blind person to do is to use a typewriter (the first ones were placed on the market in 1874), but in 1839 Braille met with success in developing a system by which a stylus and series of dots were used to draw the letters. He named this system Raphigraphy.

While Braille was trying so hard to improve reading and writing methods for blind people, society, unfortunately, was slow to catch up with him. While pupils at the Institution studied Braille's dot system sometimes unofficially in their courses and sometimes on their own initiative outside the classroom, the official method of the school was the old embossed letter method of Valentin Haüy. There may have been several reasons for this strong resistance to change: Those who had the power to abandon the old method of instruction may have been overly cautious and conservative, but it must also

be remembered that they were constantly receiving letters from all sorts of people who were convinced that they had invented a method for teaching the blind to read. Most of these inventions proved useless. Then too, abandoning the old method would mean throwing out all of the books which had been so difficult for the Institution to have printed in the first place. Perhaps another reason for not adopting Braille's writing may have been fear on the part of the sighted instructors of the new ways of teaching they themselves would have to learn. Also, with the introduction of a system with which blind teachers could function as well as the sighted, the sighted teachers would lose their sense of superiority. While Pignier had been in favor of the acceptance of Braille's writing, Dufau, who became director in 1840, was afraid that its use would further isolate the blind from the rest of the world. The French Ministry of the Interior, which made the final decision as to the "official" method of reading for the blind, believed Braille was to be encouraged in his research, but they were not ready for a formal change in systems.

However, when the Institution for Blind Youth moved to a new building in 1843, at the inauguration ceremonies Braille's system was praised before a large audience. (By this time Dufau had changed his mind and was willing to accept the dot method.) Louis Braille was deeply moved by this tribute. Furthermore, with this event began the acceptance of the braille alphabet.

All during these years, Braille's illness had brought him periods of weakness and even hemorrhaging alternating with relatively good health. By December, 1851 his health began to fail drastically. However, Braille, a deeply religious person, felt that his mission on earth had been fulfilled. He died on January 6, 1852, with no knowledge of the recognition which was to come to him, but secure in the feeling that his life's work had not been in vain.

Among the many tributes paid him, Helen Keller, herself deaf and blind since infancy, wrote:

Out of my personal experience I give deepest thanks for Louis Braille, who dropped upon the Sahara of blindness his gift of inexhaustible fertility and joy. . . . Were it not for the braille method of reading and writing, the world of the blind would be quite drab—worse than for the seeing without inkprint books. The blind are subject to countless restraints and restrictions and work alone is not sufficient to make them forget the curtailments they endure. Few who see are able or willing to read aloud to them any length of time.

Blind From Birth

I've learned from my twin daughters that a brave spirit and heart full of love can rise above any handicap

My twin daughters, Patsy and Susan, are bright, pretty teenagers who are usually bubbling with fun. Yet whenever we go out to restaurants, swimming pools and other public places, we can count on drawing stares from strangers who seem to be saying (and sometimes actually *do* say), "What do *you* have to laugh about?"

This is because both of my girls are blind.

I know about as well as anyone should have to know, that most people believe blindness brings only misery and despair. There were times when I, too, believed that our family life would have to be tragic. And because I still recall so clearly the black days of the past and have lived to see our lives turn out so differently, I want to tell our story. I hope that it may help another family with a child who is blind or who has some other handicap.

I was the mother of two entirely normal boys—Bruce aged five, and Billy, two—when I again became pregnant. By the fifth month I began to suspect that I was going to have twins, but my obstetrician did not agree with me and I was not given the X-ray examination which would have confirmed my guess. During the seventh month, while my doctor was out of town, I went into labor (which probably could have been halted if the hospital had known I was doubly pregnant) and gave birth to perfectly formed twin girls. Because they were "preemies," weighing only three pounds each, they were placed in an incubator and given oxygen. This was then the accepted medical practice all over the United States.

After six weeks the girls were mine to take home. I threw myself into a round-the-clock schedule of three-hour feedings, making formulas and caring for my husband and two boys. As we had planned before the twins came along, I also tackled a new teaching job to increase the family income.

At first, the babies were so tiny that they slept most of the time, except when they were being fed or cuddled. It did not seem strange to me or to my pediatrician that they almost always kept their eyes shut.

But after about four months, I began to notice that neither girl seemed to turn toward me when I spoke. When I mentioned this to my pediatrician, he shrugged it off as normal for preemies and told me not to worry.

I did worry though. Finally I took the babies to his office and insisted that he examine their eyes. When he did so, he could not conceal his shock. "My God, you're right!" he exclaimed. "There *is* something wrong. You should get them to an eye specialist right away."

The memory of the morning the twins were seen by the ophthalmologist has never left me. He examined them quickly; then turned to me. "They're both blind," he said. "We don't know what causes it and we don't know what to do about it. All we know—and you must know it, too —is that there is no cure."

At this time, the condition which affected the girls' eyes was causing mounting concern in medical circles. It was called "retrolental fibroplasia," and it appeared in premature babies between the second and fifth months after birth. Every newborn that weighed three pounds or less was a potential victim of this mysterious ailment. I later learned that the eyesight of thousands of infants was destroyed or damaged before doctors finally discovered—that was in 1954 —that the oxygen used in hospital incubators sometimes burned the blood vessels of the eyes. In the case of Patsy and Susan, enough vision was left in one eye for them to be aware of strong light, but both were —and are—legally, educationally and medically blind.

For more than a year after I heard the specialist's words I was in a state of shock. I can't remember much about that time except that I know I could not stop crying whenever I talked to anyone about the girls. Neither I nor my husband could bring ourselves to do any thinking or planning for the future. Instead of facing up to our problem, we tried to blot it out of our minds. My way was to plunge into work. I kept on teaching (my mother-in-law watched the babies during the day) and after school I rushed home to do my marketing, housework, cooking, caring for the children and preparing for the next day's classes.

When Susan and Patsy were near-

ly two years old a visitor appeared at our home who was to change our lives. Looking back on that afternoon now, I doubt that any door-to-door salesman ever ran into a rougher reception. As soon as I heard the words "I'm from the State School for the Blind . . ." I started to slam the door in his face. A wave of terror swept over me as my mind whirled with the thought: *He's come to take away my babies!*

But I hung onto my tongue and my visitor quietly explained why he had come: There was such an increase in the number of blind infants in the state that the school had decided to start a summer instruction workshop for parents. He had come to invite me to attend the sessions and to bring my girls with me.

My fear turned to anger. I wanted to scream at him to get out of my house. The very idea that anyone would link my family with blindness in general made me feel insulted. The suggestion that *my* children be brought to an institution along with other blind children was somehow infuriating.

"I'll listen to what you have to say," I told the man icily, "but I can tell you right now you're wasting your time. I wouldn't be interested."

We sat down in the living room and for the next two hours I was as disagreeable as it's possible to be. I thought of a thousand excuses why the girls couldn't leave home and why I couldn't spare the time for such a project. But finally—and I thank God for it now—my visitor's patience, tact and logic won out. I agreed to attend the session and bring the twins with me.

The two weeks we spent at the workshop that summer left me physically and emotionally exhausted. (No wonder, since I was straining every nerve to absorb all I heard and at the same time to appear calmly aloof.) But during those weeks, I learned the most valuable lesson of my life: *It is no kindness to handicapped children to shut them off from the world or to pretend*

that their handicap doesn't exist. The most important thing for parents is to be able to accept their problem without shame or guilt and to take positive steps to help their child grow up as happily as possible.

As soon as I was home again with Patsy and Susan, my husband and I set about transforming our house into a safe place for our blind babies. We cut tennis balls in half and taped them over every sharp corner of furniture. We put everything that was breakable or could cause injury out of their reach. Thus, instead of being restricted to a room or a playpen like so many blind children, the girls had the whole house as their nursery.

Previously they had tended to avoid creeping or walking. Now we turned them loose to roam, to creep, to crawl, to touch, to feel, to smell, to taste, to listen. We hung swings in the yard so that they could exercise and gain a sense of balance, and erected hang bars indoors so that they could strengthen their arms and shoulders. (Many blind children, I had learned at school, have such weak arm and torso muscles from lack of exercise that they even find it hard to operate a Braille typewriter.)

We filled their lives with toys that were soft and pleasing to the touch and made interesting sounds. The more they resembled the real thing, the better. We played games with them—hide-and-seek and what-is-it —in which we gave them something to hold while we told them its name and how it was used. Since they could not see a smile, we went out of our way to put warmth and encouragement into our voices and to avoid harsh tones.

When the girls were quite young, they would stop and remain absolutely quiet if they were reprimanded or told not to do something. One day —they must have been about four at the time—the girls came through the living room carrying pans of water which they were going to take outside and dump into a flower bed. As they started back through the house to refill their pans, I called out to them to stop. They stood still for a few moments and then began tiptoeing past me.

and games. At times both girls have felt frustrated and defeated and angry. Straining to learn without sight is extremely tiring and they sometimes become waspish with fatigue and nervous strain.

There have also been times when practical jokes and cruel remarks

have made them miserable.

On one occasion Patsy lost her way while she was on a shopping trip downtown and, alone and frightened on a strange street, she inadvertently stepped in front of a car. There was a screech of tires and then, close to her face, a man's angry voice: "People like you ought to stay off the streets. You're a menace, that's what you are!"

For every hurt and rebuff, however, there have been a hundred times as much laughter. I once came home and found Susan and her friends collapsed with the giggles. Shopping in a downtown store, she had bought a Coke and had been standing at the top of an escalator, sipping it out of a container, when a man who was riding up the stairs saw her cane and what appeared to him to be a cup. The next thing she knew he had dropped a handful of coins in her Coke. "The way I yelled, 'Oh, no!' will probably haunt that poor man for months!" said Susan.

And even though a stranger once called her a menace, Patsy and her sister continue to love people and to do everything in their power to make others happy.

Not long ago, Susan walked fifteen blocks by herself to our local hospital, only to announce: "It's a beautiful day! Does anybody around here need a visitor?"

The other day someone asked her how she thought parents can best help a blind child. Without a moment's hesitation she answered, "For goodness sake, don't lead them around! Quit acting as if there were something wrong with them just because they can't see!" To me that brisk, matter-of-fact reply is a tribute—and a reassurance—beyond all price.

"Remember now," I said. "Don't take any more water outside."

Again they stopped in their tracks, and Patsy said in a puzzled tone, "Did you *hear* us?"

"No," I replied.

"Then how did you know what we were doing?"

I tried to explain I could "see" without having to hear or touch. Patsy stomped her foot and walked away, exclaiming indignantly, "It isn't fair!" From that day we began

to talk to them about their handicap, helping them to understand, without self-pity, that they were different.

Meanwhile, my husband and I were resisting pressure to send them away to a boarding school for the blind. As much as I had learned from the teachers at the State School's summer session, I still felt a child belonged in his own home.

But kindergarten in public school turned out to be a discouraging setback. The classes were large and the busy teachers couldn't give my girls the time and attention they needed. I was asked to withdraw them.

I gritted my teeth. "All right," I said, "but they'll be back. You can count on that."

I went to see the director of the School for the Blind, who by that time had become my friend. I told him what had happened.

"I know how much you want Sue and Patsy home with you," he said, "but I have a suggestion. In the fall, let them come to us for just one school year. We'll give them first-grade training and teach them how to get along in a regular school later."

The school was about 150 miles upstate from our home. Even though I couldn't live with Sue and Patsy, I quit my job and moved into a room in the same town so that I could spend evenings and weekends with them. Between visits, I shuttled back and forth to our home to keep the rest of the family going. It was one of our toughest years, but we managed it.

The following September we went back for another try at public school. This time the girls made it. Each day they had a lesson in Braille from a specialist, but, except for that, they were in regular classes. They have been public school children ever since.

Over the years, both have learned Braille typing as well as Braille reading. They use talking records for their studies and listen to recorded books and magazines. (When the pace gets too slow for them, they turn up their phonographs to double speed. Noises that sound like Donald Duck gibberish to us make perfect sense to their trained ears!)

Only when you work with blind children do you realize how many seemingly instinctive gestures and expressions actually depend on eyesight. For example, it doesn't come

naturally for a blind person to turn in the direction of someone he's talking to. The twins do it now, but only after many months of long and sometimes stormy practice. Similarly, we've worked on the business of smiling—what is a smile? When do you do it? What kinds are there? And how do you raise your eyebrows? Why?

Both Patsy and Susan have always wanted to jump, run, dance and skip the way their friends did and we encouraged them to do it. Inevitably there would be collisions with furniture, with visitors, with each other. Innumerable times I stood with my heart in my throat, aching to prevent them from taking chances, yet knowing that they had to do it. And they knew it too. Not so long ago, Patsy said as much to me. "Thank you, Mommy, for letting us fall," she said. These words were music to my ears.

By the time the girls were nine years old they could do almost everything their friends could do. They ran, swam, dived, walked to school and took buses downtown by themselves. They were equally at ease on a trampoline, and in Sunday school. They learned to make their own beds, take care of their rooms, cook on an electric stove, set the table, do the dishes and put them away.

They also have become very clothes conscious and, in true teenage fashion, spend hours talking to their schoolmates about what to wear and why; what colors are most becoming; what lines are best for their figures. Their sensitive fingers have taught them a lot about fabrics and they've acquired strong likes and dislikes on the subject. As they explain it to me, they "sort of feel" colors, too. "If I wear a blue dress," Susan says, "I picture myself in blue all that day."

Now that they're seniors in high school, they've begun putting their hair up in rollers and making a point of getting their lipstick on straight. They're likely to saunter out from their rooms with a new twist or flip which leaves me blinking. From informal picnics and neighborhood parties, they've moved along to dating and going to dances.

Camp Challenge: A Preschool Program for Visually Handicapped Children and Their Parents

By Jean Grogan M.Ed. and Sheldon Maron Ph.D.

While Camp Challenge is designed primarily for children with visual disabilities, it is a model that can be adapted to provide an effective program for all children with disabilities and their families.

Camp Challenge is a program for visually disabled (and multiply-disabled) preschool children and their parents. It began in 1973 as a cooperative venture between the Bureau of Blind Services (part of the Florida State Department of Education) and the Visual Disabilities Track (part of the Special Education Program) at Florida State University. The camp itself is owned and operated by the Easter Seal Society of Florida.

The camp's purpose is threefold: 1) to provide direct services to visually disabled preschoolers and their parents; 2) to serve as a resource for parents and professionals who care for such children and who seek preschool services for them; and 3) to provide practical experience in a unique setting for Florida State University students majoring in visual disabilities (and related areas).

The program is conducted twice yearly — in October and in April. Each session runs for five days and is funded by the Bureau of Blind Services (BBS). The camp is located in a picturesque setting in central Florida, close to the city of Orlando.

From twenty-seven to thirty families attend each session. Families are referred by BBS caseworkers who recommend that they submit applications to the state BBS office or to us at Florida State University. In the past two years we have been unable to accept all the applications for Camp Challenge, the need for such a service has been so great. In January 1976, a BBS study indicated that there are more than 250 visually handicapped preschoolers in Florida, many of whom receive few or no services.

To accommodate as many families as possible, we give first priority to those who have not previously participated in Camp Challenge. Occasionally an "alumnus" is accepted, especially if he or she has shown signs of development regression over the past year. Moreover, some families should return, particularly families from rural areas where there are no preschool or infant stimulation programs and those with more severely disabled children.

At least one parent, guardian or foster parent must accompany each child. Each session begins on a Saturday and is concluded on the following Thursday; this weekend start has enabled a number of fathers to attend. We try to encourage both parents to participate whenever possible because the growth and development of children with disabilities requires the support and participation of both parents, especially in the early years. All too often fathers are not involved to the degree that is necessary, leaving an awesome burden for the mother to bear alone.

In the past, 35 per cent of all our families have had both parents in attendance at camp — a good percentage considering that most fathers and some mothers miss a week of work, and salary, in order to participate in the program.

The Parents' Program

The camp program is comprised of two distinct, simultaneous subprograms, one for the parents and one for the children. The parents' program includes a series of demonstrations, simulations of visual limitations and discussions by professionals from a wide variety of disciplines and settings (see chart). Parents are divided into small groups to maximize participation and individual attention. In addition, a nightly program for parents (see chart) includes speakers, movies, seminars, project demonstrations, and the like, designed to enhance

15

1. AN OVERVIEW

Parents' Daily Program

Monday

9:00 a.m.	The Handicapped Child in the Family — Dealing with Emotional Problems
11:00	Promoting Motor Development in Preschool Blind Children
12:00	Lunch (parents eat under blindfold)
1:00 p.m.	Rest hour
2:00	Common Eye Disorders in Young Children
3:00	Orientation and Mobility Simulation — Basic Sighted Guide Techniques
8:00	Feedback session from daily program. Crafts program: Parents make educational toys. Teachers demonstrate toys.

Tuesday

9:00 a.m.	Developing Readiness Skills — Emphasis on Parent-made Materials
11:00	Teaching Feeding Skills
12:00	Lunch
1:00 p.m.	Rest hour
2:00	Parents Observations of Teachers and Students Working with Children
3:30	Demonstration of Educational Materials Commercially Available
8:00	Feedback session from daily program. Demonstration on Teaching Dressing Skills.

Child's Daily Program

Time	Group 1	Group 2
9:00 - 10:00	Physical Education	Sensory Stimulation
10:00 - 11:00	Sensory Stimulation	Swimming
11:00 - 12:00	Swimming	Nature
12:00 - 1:00	Lunch	Lunch
1:00 - 2:00	Rest hour	Rest hour
2:00 - 3:00	Nature	Crafts
3:00 - 4:00	Crafts	Physical Education

parents' understanding of their children's situation.

The programs are designed to give parents practical information that can help them to help their child. For instance, after the presentation on readiness skills (social and academic skills that help prepare the child for school), the parents are given an opportunity to construct materials to use later with their own children. These toys are made from common materials found at home such as egg cartons, fabric scraps, rice, etc. Each parent has a chance to try his "finished product" with his child during the course of the week. These skills and methods will continue to be useful after they have returned home.

Some parents participate in panel discussions in which they have an opportunity to offer their experiences and ideas concerning the special care their children require. These panels stimulate discussions among all parents present.

Parents also spend one morning during the session in nearby Orlando where they observe a local public school program (with well-equipped resource rooms) for visually disabled children of elementary school age. Parents get a reassuring firsthand glimpse of programs many of their children will soon be entering. While there, parents have ample opportunity to talk with teachers and get further suggestions regarding the readiness skills their children need to develop before entering school.

As the week progresses, friendships are made and parents usually find themselves exchanging addresses, toys, children's clothes, etc. Shortly after the close of camp, a list of addresses of camp participants is sent to each family.

On the last day of each session, each family is asked to complete an evaluation of the camp program. These evaluations are carefully tabulated to enable us to make modifications and improvements in the program.

The philosophy at Camp Challenge emphasizes the similarities of our children to all children . . .

The Children's Program

The children's program is conducted concurrently with the parents' program. Approximately thirty children are divided as evenly as possible into five groups. The groups are staffed by twelve teacher-consultants (certified workers with the visually handicapped) and eighteen Florida State University students so that the child-staff ratio is just about one to one. This ratio is necessary because of the increasing number of young children and severely multiply-disabled children who attend. In addition, the Easter Seal Society provides a full-time swimming instructor, camp director and cooks.

On the first day of camp the staff administers a battery of tests to each child to assess skills in motor development, communication and daily living skills (feeding, dressing, grooming, etc.). For example, each child is tested to ascertain his ability to indicate the need to use the bathroom, to roll independently from stomach to back, and to use facial and bodily gestures to indicate wants and needs. This information, together with direct observations, parent conversations and background information from application forms, determines the individualized instructional program for the next four and one-half days. A teacher-consultant may already have worked with some of the children, and this familiarity helps provide more comprehensive planning.

The children's program (see chart) involves activities based on the child's needs. Teachers in each group, together with students and in . consultation with us, formulate the program for each session. For some children the program may include learning to focus attention and to make basic responses of acknowledgement. For others it may involve gross motor activities (crawling, walking, running, etc.), toileting and mastering skills of daily living (feeding and dressing). For still others, developing fine motor skills (manual dexterity) and utilizing residual vision (as well as hearing, touch and smell) may be taught.

Parents spend one afternoon observing the teacher-consultants and the students working with their children. Before the close of camp, each family meets with the staff members who have worked with their child. At this time, specific objectives and recommendations are made to parents. The staff suggests activities, materials and procedures to help the child meet these objectives. A comprehensive written report is sent to the appropriate BBS caseworker so that the objectives established at camp can be worked on and realized at home. Parents have access to the report through their caseworker.

Objectives

We realize that objectives must be limited in a five-day program. On the other hand, we never cease to be amazed at the progress that can be made even in this short period of time. With an intensive stimulation program, children have made significant gains in growth and development. The prognosis for these children becoming as independent as they can be improves significantly if intervention programs begin long before school age.

While the children's program represents a short-term source of help, the parents' program represents a continuing resource worth far more than the time spent at Camp Challenge. Parents are not only referred to specific personnel and agencies to contact back home, but, more important, they learn that they can play a crucial role in their child's growth and development.

A great deal can be done if begun early enough to eliminate the negative emotional connotations of blindness and the stereotype of dependency that blindness conveys to the public — including parents of children who are visually disabled. The camp program stresses the idea that while a visual handicap does imply certain restrictions and/or special provisions, a visually handicapped child is a *child* first, with needs similar to those of *all* children. He or she goes through the same developmental sequences and stages as all children. Vision problems are usually not only conspicuous, they often reinforce parents' perceptions that their child is somehow "different." The philosophy at Camp Challenge emphasizes the similarities of our children to all children, disabled or not: we build on these common aspects of growth and development. If we do this, we build on strengths not weaknesses, and that is the cornerstone of a sound educational program.

Seeing The Blind As They 'See' Us

PATRICIA FOX SHEINWOLD

Musician/performer Stevie Wonder and well-known labor columnist Victory Riesel are both blind, but with a difference. Wonder, blind from birth, may feel what the color blue looks like but, given instant sight, he'd never recognize it. Risel, blinded in mid-life by acid-throwing mobsters, as the color imprinted on his brain from his early, sighted days. Were his vision restored, chances are he could point to it istantly.

Along with about 500,000 other Americans, both men are classified as officially blind. In legalese, this means they have "20/200 visual acuity or less in the "better' eye, with correcting glasses, or whose widest diameter of visual field subtends an angular distance no greater than 20 degrees." In everyday life, however, it may mean having to turn to a dog or a stranger just to cross the street.

In this article, author Patricia Fox Sheinwold, who has worked intimately with the blind, explains the deep desire of the blind to live normally. And she shows how you the sighted can help them to make it in the world instead of sitting home in isolation the rest of their days.

From time to time, we are shown fragmented stories on TV about the blind going to school to get a dog or a cane, or learning to read and write braille. But we don't see what happens after that person goes home. What happens day after day after day? We, the public, are never "Let in" on the routine living of the persons with whom we have just spent a videotaped hour, much less the emotional part of thieir lives.

The blind do go home, they do continue to live. But the majority do not have the exciting, sometimes glamorous life as depicted on TV about Helen Keller, pianist-composer Alec Templeton, or other famous blind people. Instead, it's down to basics or how to get on with it.

In the United States (Puerto Rico and the Virgin Islands inclusive), the official count of legally blind for 1976 came to 490,200 — one out of 400. Of that total, 45,750 became blind in 1976 alone.

In terms of causes, there are two main definitions of blindness: congenital blindness, dating from birth; and acquired blidness, a loss of sight caused by injury, accident or disease.

Cataracts, glaucoma and trachoma are some of the diseases causing blindness; in elderly people the most common one is diabetes.

Whatever the cause, these poeple must be assimilated into the mainstream of life. Across the country there are schools, institutions, government agencies, radio stations individuals, all helping the cause — and you, the person in the street, willing to help too. But, often, the willingess to help a stranger is not quite enough.

Recently, for example, I saw a sighted woman trying to help an unsighted man cross a street. It was a sight. The woman who could see took the arm of the blind man and pushed him in front; with this maneuver, the blind man was actually doing the leading. The intention was good, but the result could have been disastrous.

If you are ever in this situation, offer your arm to the blind person. Now, with his hand securely on your upper arm, both of you will cross the street safely. Don't be afraid to be positive. A blind person needs positive ess because this relays security; it is always security he searches for. And don't be hesitant or withhold your desire to help.

The Importance Of Order

A synonym for security is certainty. The humdrum details of everyday living are enlarged in the world of the sightless unless there is certainty. If a blind person is to have the freedom of dressing alone, the procedure can be simple so long as his clothing is returned each time to the same place. Maintaining order is a prime requisite of certainty. Colors are kept to a minimum -- only white shirts and black socks, for example. This way, the person can grab a shirt or a pair of socks without the danger of being mismatched or wearing clownlike colors. Instead of hanging on the customary tie rack, neckwear can be draped around the hangers of matching suits. A blind man tires of the same tie just as a sighted man does, so a choice is deisrable. He switches according to the feel of the material and opts for smooth days, coarse days, silky or linen days, depending upon his humor.

Assurance is another synonym for security. When the blind sit down to eat, assurance is what they want. What they do not want is the jolt of an unexpected food item going into their mouths. If a plate is said to contain steak and string beans, it shouldn't contain roast beef and pea pods. We the sighted look at food and make our mental judgments which are, in turn, transferred to our palates. In a twinkling, we have visually and mentally discarded anything we do not want before starting to eat. A blind person, of course, is unable to do this, so jokes he can do without.

The food is put on the plate in clockwise order: steak at 12 o'clock, peas at 3, potatoes at 6, etc. There are no statistics to explain why some will cut up their own food and some will not. But the consensus of opinion is that those with acquired blindness, weo've had the chance to actually use a knife while learning to wield it are more confident than the born-blind, who tne to be hesitant.

Uses Of Braille

Safety is aonother symonym for security, and the American Foundation for the Blind has come up with some extraordinary products to help in making everyday routine safer. All kinds of cooking utensils marked in braille enable the blind to measure accurately and cook efficiently.

Additionally, there are products which safeguard. The ordinary 3x5 index cards are treated with a covering which inusres the wirter of braille that once the tiny dots are put on the card they will not crush or be destroyed. Even the United States Postal Service cannot push down the tiny brailled dots. There is also a braille labeling device. Imagine what this means to a blind person.

He can label his records, tapes, files, books, even luggage — and never again does he have to ask, "l sthis Barbra Streisand or Jascha Heifetz?" One young housewife has found another use for the labeler. She labels all the leftover food containers in the fridge. "This way," she says, "my husband doesn't stick his fingers in everything until he finds the chocolate pudding."

Scurity, certainty, assurance, safety: the cornerstones of the blind, combined with the readily available products so necessary and so useful. Armed with these — plus the cooperation and caring of the sighted world -- the blind are on their way.

A surprising number of them not only make it in everyday living; they make it big. People like entertainer Stevie Wonder for example.

He walks onto the stage with assistance. He sits down at the piano and, within minutes, his incredible spirit, the excitement he generates in performance, the ease with which he does it catches the audience and keeps them glued to their seats for two hours. But it is more than his extraordinary talent. It's an aura; and, within that aura, there is an acceptance. He is blind but he makes you forget it.

The blind from birth speak about two worlds, the sighted world and the unsighted world. They knwo there is a difference, but they are blessed because they do not really know the difference. The adventitiously blind person, one who has been accidentally blinded, has seen; so, when his sight, is lost, he knows the difference, Obviously, the emtional makeup and problems between the two are varied and complex.

Images

A congenitally blind person knows, for example, about baseball. He knows the rules of the game, the sounds of the game — and some, perhaps, have held a bat, mitt or ball so they would know the feel of the game. But close your eyes — you who are sighted can see the vastness of the diamond, the players strung across the outfield and infield, the dugout, the batter, and you can see a runner going from base to base — all with your eyes closed. Therein lies the difference. Having never had sight, Stevie Wonder and others like him cannot envision this; but, in exchange they have a sort of built-in protection: they do not miss what they have never known. When they speak of the two worlds, it is with ease and graciousness.

The acentitiously blind person holds imprinted on his brain all that he saw before the loss of sight. Let's say that he has watched a game of baseball. When the sport is mentioned, he can conjure up the entire image. But he knows the loss. He also has a set of built-in fears. He knows what it looks like from the top of a flight of stairs and he can imagine falling. He therefore is quite cautious. A born-blind person does not know this and usually flies up and down staircases fearlessly. When it comes to Stevie Wonder's performance, a great part of his ease can be attributed to his never having had sight — hence, there is no distraction from loss. This may sound like an oversimplification, but the basic difference matters.

Dreaming illustrates still another difference. Those who have had sight can, in their dreams, use visual imprints already on the brain. The born blind, however, dream by sound and touch only.

For instance, a born-blind person can readily distinguish an ashtray from a saucer or glass from a cup — by touch. But with instant sight it is doubtful if he would know the ashtray from the saucer or the cup from the glass.

What Is Color?

Then there is the matter of color. For years, I had heard a blind friend talk easily of color. He would remark, "The sky must be very gray with the approaching storm"; or, "What a beautiful bright day — the sky must be as blue as can be." It never occurred to me to question this. Then, after five years of friendship, we were fishing one day off the coast of Cape Cod. My friend had just landed a big one and wanted me to see it.

He found me in the stern of the boat watching the sunset. Without any hesitation, I launched into a description of the magnificent colors. Long ago, I'd been put at ease by him and had no reason to think about guarding my words. Imagine my surprise, then, when forgetting all about the fish, he sat down next to me and asked intently, "What is color?"

After a moment of thought, I chose the parallel of music to explain color but prefaced by saying it was only my interpretation. Someone else could differ. Debussy's "La Mer" makes me think of blue, while Stravinsky's "Firebird" reminds me of red and orange. "Star Dust" conjures up yellow and "God Bless America" makes me think green. However, the choices are very personal.

The emotional makeup of a blind person is the determining factor when or if he chooses a dog, a cane or a human. With the first two, he can free himself from bondage. If he relies on another person, he may feel safer but he surely isn't free.

After World War I, shepherd dogs were being trained in Germany as guides for blinded veterans (today golden and Labrador retrievers are also used, as well as individual dogs of other breeds). This came to the attention of Dorothy Harrison Eustis of Philadelphia, who at the time was living in Switzerland. She was initially interested in scientific breeding of German shepherd dogs for desirable character traits: alertness, responsibility and stamina. She and her staff realized that the effectiveness of the breeding program could be measured only by the dogs' performance of responsible tasks, so a training program was also developed.

When Ms. Eustis visited the school in Germany, she became aware of the dogs' full potential. An article she authored on "The Seeing Eye" came to the notice of Morris Frank, a blind Tennessean. He wrote to Ms. Eustis: "Thousands of blind like me abhor being dependent on others. Help me and I will help them. Train me and I will bring back my dog and show people here how a blind man can be absolutely on his own."

Morris Frank went to Switzerland; he received a dog and both were trained there. Ms. Eustis returned to the United States along with Mr. Frank and his dog, and the first "seeing-eye" class was held in Nashville, Tenn. In 1929, two members were in attendance. Today there are many schools, among them: Guide Dogs,

Inc., in San Raphael, Calif.; Pilot Dogs in Columbus, Ohio; Leader Dogs in Rochester, Mich.; and Seeing Eye in Morristown, N.J.

The schools vary in their approach to fees or non-fees. Seeing Eye asks the blind person to assume an obligation of $150 toward adjustment with a first dog and a nominal fee in obtaining a replacement dog. However, no one has ever been denied a Seeing Eye dog because of a lack of funds. The school feels that payments "represent dignity and self-respect to the student."

Guide Dogs asks no payment: "We make no charge to the blind for the protection of the animal. The school offers conveniences and advantages which continue after the student and dog have gone home. By retaining ownership of the animal, Guide Dogs can insure that the dogs are used for the purposes for which they were trained." Graduates of Guide Dogs repay in other ways. One, a West Coast rancher, sends apples; another continually supplies the school with chickens; yet another, British-born jazz pianist George Shearing, donates the proceeds from yearly benefits.

Other schools across the country run the gamut from the seeing Eye point of view to the Guide Dogs approach. And, as an alternative to the dog guide, there is the cane.

Perfecting The Cane

After World War II, a young doctor, Richard Hoover, returned to Hines, Ill., determined to perfect a cane method for blinded veterans. Until then, sort walking sticks had been used. Dr. Hoover's long "white cane" is now very familiar, and his method is known as the Hoover Method. In 1931, a federal law was passed decreeing that the "white cane" means right-of-way.

The canes are made of aluminum covered with white Scotlite at the top and red Scotlite below. Both glimmer in the dark. The size varies; each cane is made to reach one inch above the owner's sternum.

The fee for training, where one exists, is generally nominal. The Lighthouse in New York City, for instance, charges $9.95, a fee that includes cane as well as instruction. However, nobody has ever been denied entrance for lack of funds.

Training requires six weeks, every day, and is done on a one-to-one basis. The basics are the same: the cane is moved from left to right in an arc-like, two-point touch, which warns the user two steps ahead. In a familiar environment, it is moved diagonally in front of the person.

After basic training, each student is taught how the cane can be adapted to his own needs. A student in New York City, for example, would have to have subway training, while another who is in college in Iowa would need training for school mobility.

But why a dog instead of a cane or vice versa? Although the average life span of dog guides is 10 years, they do die. Cane users prefer not to face this, even though they know they can return to the school for a new dog. Some students have had as many as three or four dogs and a few have returned for a fifth.

Persons with dog guides feel that the effort and even the sadness is worth it, not only because of the freedom but because of the companionship and love they receive from their dogs. The cane schools recommend both; for, if and when the dog dies or is sick, the blind person still has mobility.

Guide Dogs is always enthusiastic if a person comes to school having had cane training, which sets a good foundation for work with a dog. One woman came to Guide Dogs at age 70 for her first dog after relying on a cane for 20 years. When the school followed upon her progress, the question was asked, "What is the difference between using the cane and the dog?" She replied: "I never fell in love with a cane."

Both cane and dog schools have their share of dropouts. The emotional factor plays an important part. There is anxiety, there is fear, there is proof of blindness when using a cane or dog that people not born blind can picture and won't accept.

Flying Blind

No matter how much you read about a subject or try to learn at first hand the problems of others, there is no substitute for experience.

When I boarded a 747 en route from Los Angeles to New York, I was wearing sunglasses and holding a harness strapped to the back of my German shepherd. I wasn't intentionally trying to do the airlines out of its fee for the dog; but I was afraid of crating her to be left willy-nilly in the belly of the plane, where sometimes the heat goes off or the oxygen supply diminishes. And even though I've spent 20 years around the blind, I wanted firsthand experience.

Having observed dog-guide procedure, I knew enough to release the harness, hold the leash in my hand and take the arm of a sighted person. With the harness released, the dog is not working. My dog looked the part, was very well trained, but could heel not guide. With me on the seat and the dog snuggled underneath, we began our five-hour flight cross-country.

I was not prepared for the well-meaning assistance of fellow passengers and crew — inexperienced as it was. Once we were aloft, the stewardess asked if I wanted to see the movie; then, horrified at what she had said, she covered her mouth with her hand. She had used the word "see."

But in the language of the blind, the word see is perfectly acceptable, even preferred. Any sidestepping of it only points up that the person is different. Asking someone if he's heard the Johnny Carson show is a bit clumsy.

After the stewardess had recovered from her discomfort about the movie, I gently reminded her that I could hear and

would enjoy a headset. She did not ask for the customary $2 charge. I felt different.

The lady seated to my right struck up a conversation by admiring the dog; but she, too, thought I was deaf. For a few seconds, I wondered how to tell her diplomatically, but the onslaught in the right ear made me just do it. What she had done was make me aware that all of us inadvertently think one affliction breeds another.

Dinner was served after the movie and my flying companion offered to help. I asked her to please tell me what was on the plate and its location. But in her zealous effort when she lifted my hand, she plunked it on top of the grapefruit and then into the coffee, saying as she did it,, "This is grapefruit and this is coffee." Two of my fingers got burned and three got very sticky. Now she knew that, besides not being deaf, I had feeling in my hands. This was catalogued for future reference: just barley touch the top of the objects if the blind person needs to be shown.

When we were about an hour out of New York, I asked her to escort me to the lavatory.

Emotional Impact

Once inside, alone, I removed the dark glasses and began to cry. I had no idea of the emotional impact involved. Any guilt feelings were long since gone — all that remained was the desire to pass along everything and anything I was learning from this experience. Perhaps it's not necessary to say this, but I feel I must: In no way was I trying to ridicule anyone with whom I came in contact while traveling, nor in any way to demean the blind, many of whome are dear friends.

When the plane touched the ground, my companion asked me one last question. She was nervous — I could tell by the quiver in her voice.

"Which do you think is worse — to be blind or deaf?"

I answered by quoting a blind frined. He had said this to me on the day of his adopted daughter's first birthday:

"I would like to see the sky, water, trees, and all of God's wondrous works, and I would like to see my child. But in not seeing, I can still hear the rain flowing from the sky, the water slashing against the house during a storm. I can hear the trees bowing and bending from the wind, and best of all, I can hear my daughter

THE WHITE CANE

Kenneth Jernigan, President of the National Federation of the Blind since 1968 and Director of the Iowa Commission for the Blind since 1958.

A white cane in our society has become one of the symbols of a blind person's ability to come and go on his own. Its use has promoted courtesy and opportunity for mobility for the blind on our streets and highways. To make the American people more fully aware of the meaning of the white cane, and of the need for motorists to exercise special care for the blind persons who carry it, Congress, by a joint resolution approved October 6, 1964, authorized the President to proclaim October 15 of each year as White Cane Safety Day.

Now, therefore, I, Lyndon B. Johnson, President of the United States of America, do hereby proclaim October 15, 1964, as White Cane Safety Day.

That Presidential proclamation marked the climax of an historic campaign by the organized blind to gain recognition by the states and the nation of the rights of blind pedestrians. It was in 1930 that the first state law was passed requiring motorists to stop when a blind person crossed the street with a white cane. Today white cane laws are on the books of every state in the Union, providing blind persons a legal status in traffic by virtually wiping out the traditional assumption of contributory negligence on the part of blind pedestrians in the event of accident. William Taylor, a blind attorney from Pennsylvania, became the acknowledged leader and publicist of the NFB's white cane activities.

The white cane is therefore a symbol of equality [said Jacobus tenBroek in a 1960 speech]. *And still more it is clearly a sign of mobility. In the routines of daily living, as at a deeper social level, the keynote of our way of life is mobility: the capacity to get around, to move at a normal pace in step with the passing parade. In this race, until very recently, the blind were clearly lagging and falling ever farther behind . . . But today the blind of America are catching up. Just as they are gaining social and economic mobility through the expansion of vocational horizons, so they are achieving a new freedom of physical mobility through the expansion of legal opportunities centering upon the White Cane Laws.*

In addition to working for federal and state enactments protecting the right of passage by blind pedestrians, the Federation has sought in other ways to increase public recognition of the values symbolized by the white cane. In 1947, the NFB established the third week in May as a period for special concentration on efforts to educate the public concerning the hopes and aspirations of the blind and to ask their support. White Cane Week is a cooperative effort of the National Federation and its affiliates, during which millions of envelopes have been mailed across the land enclosing a pamphlet emphasizing the ability of the blind to be independent.

>   *For blind people everywhere* [as Dr. tenBroek said]
>   *the white cane is not a badge of difference—but a token of*
>   *their equality and integration. And for those who know its*
>   *history and associations, the white cane is also something*
>   *more: it is the tangible expression not only of mobility, but*
>   *of a movement.*
>
>   *It is indeed appropriate that the organized move-*
>   *ment of the National Federation of the Blind should have*
>   *as its hallmark this symbol of the white cane . . . During the*
>   *decade following the introduction of the white cane, state-*
>   *wide organizations began to emerge in numbers across the*
>   *country, in the first wave of a movement which was climaxed*
>   *by the founding of the National Federation in 1940. Through*
>   *the adoption of the White Cane Laws, the blind have gained*
>   *the legal right to travel, the right of physical mobility. And*
>   *at the same time, through the organization of their own*
>   *national and state associations, the blind have gained the*
>   *social right of movement and the rights of a social movement.*

In 1966 Dr. tenBroek published his definitive work on the subject, "The Right to Live in the World: The Disabled in the Law of Torts." Based on this analysis of existing law, the Federation developed a Model White Cane Law, which constitutes a veritable Bill of Rights for the blind. It has since been introduced in the Legislatures of more than half of the States and has been adopted in whole or in part by more than a dozen.

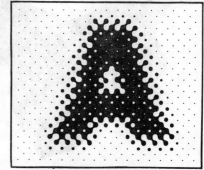

Mother's
Arms

Etiology of Visual Impairment

The human eye is a complicated organ, any part of which is susceptible to damage and disease. The eyeball itself, the cornea covering the anterior portion of it, or the lens inside, may have defects of structure or function. The conjunctiva, which surrounds the eye, may be diseased or injured. Likewise, the iris, retina, and optic nerve may be damaged so as to affect vision. Until recently the most common location of difficulty resulting in visual impairment has been the retina, due mostly to a disease known as retrolental fibroplasia, which fortunately, has had a marked decline, due to current medical technology. Studies have proven that structural anomalies of the eyeball account for nearly one-fourth of visual impairments in children.

In regards to the etiology of blindness, The National Society for the Prevention of Blindness has for many years attempted to obtain statistics on the prevalence, causes, and conditions of blindness. The major causes have been listed in broad categories as: infectious diseases, accidents, and injuries, poisonings, tumors, general diseases, and prenatal influences, including heredity. It was reported by this association that prenatal conditions account for 47.7 percent of legally blind children. Retrolental fibroplasia, a condition in which the detached retina is found floating behind the lens, accounted for 33.3 percent of legal blindness among school-age children. Infectious diseases accounted for 7 to 8 percent, and injuries, including accidents, accounted for a little over 2 percent.

Current medical technology and research continue to make clearer, the causes of visual impairment. Through improved diagnosis and assessment, stemming from a clear definition of the etiology of visual impairments, appropriate educational services may be delivered.

YOUR EYES

What the Problems Are

THOMAS CHALKLEY, M.D.

*Assistant Professor, Northwestern
University Medical School;
Member, Editorial Board of the
American Journal of Ophthalmology*

The old-fashioned box camera rarely broke down; but it could not be focused sharply, it always needed bright light, and it could only do a fraction of the things that a modern camera can do. The modern camera, with its coupled range finder, built-in light meter, and self-adjusting shutter speed and lens opening, is far more vulnerable, because it has more that can break down. So it is with our eyes. Vulnerability is part of the price we pay for increased complexity and efficiency. With all the things that can go wrong with our eyes, the amazing thing is that so few actually do.

Our eyes, like us, are mortal, and as we age, so do they. Like the rest of the body, the eyes lose efficiency as they grow older. Fortunately, the sciences of optics and ophthalmology make it possible to compensate for or correct the so-called "degenerative" changes so that, with corrective lenses, we need suffer no significant loss of vision.

Many people think that if they have 20/20 vision their eyes are about as good as they can be. This is not true. All that is meant by 20/20 vision is that at twenty feet we can see what we should be able to see at that distance. Vision rated at 20/30 means that one sees at twenty feet objects that should be clear at thirty. This system of measuring vision was developed in 1863 to be used in conjunction with the standard Snellen eye chart. It does not tell us whether our eyesight is normal; it only measures what we are able to see at twenty feet.

Some people with natural 20/20 vision could not read this page without corrective eyeglasses, and some who need glasses to achieve 20/20 vision could read this page without them. Having 20/20 vision is fine as far as it goes, but it is not enough. For normal vision, one should be able to see clearly and without strain from less than a foot away to infinity.

Care of the eyes and correction of defects in vision rests with a highly trained and skilled group of specialists. First of these is the *ophthalmologist* or *oculist*, who is a medical doctor and surgeon specially qualified to diagnose and treat diseases and defects of the eye. He is also trained to measure changes of vision, whether one is nearsighted or farsighted, and to prescribe corrective lenses.

The *optometrist* is trained and licensed to examine and measure the eyes for defects in vision, to prescribe corrective lenses, and to grind and fit them. While he does not treat diseases of the eye, he is often the first to detect them.

The third specialist is the *optician*, who is trained to grind the lenses prescribed by an ophthalmologist or optometrist, fit them properly, and provide suitable frames for eyeglasses. He does not examine the eyes for visual defects or disease, nor does he treat them.

The division of the problems of sight into two main groups, the ordinary and the extraordinary, is for the author's convenience rather than any scientifically precise distinction. "Ordinary" problems include the effects of the aging process, plus problems and defects that arise mainly from abnormalities in structure — eyeballs that are too large or too small, irregularities of the cornea or lens, defects of the orbital muscles that result in misalignment of the eyes, and so on. These have been called ordinary because they are endogenous and, to a greater or lesser degree, affect all of us. For the most part, too, they are genetically determined, but this distinction is not confined to the ordinary problems.

The "extraordinary" problems, on the other hand, are more likely to be caused by factors outside of ourselves, such as bacterial and viral infections, diseases that affect the eyes, and injuries of one sort or another. This category also includes disturbances that are by-products of various allergic conditions and such ailments as diabetes, hypertension, and gout.

For the most part, these "extraordinary" problems are not genetically influenced to the same degree as the ordinary problems, although heredity certainly plays an indirect role in some, such as diabetes, where the eye involvement is a secondary effect of the disease.

"Ordinary" Problems

Because of the structure of our lenses, two defects are built into all human eyes — *spherical aberration* and *chromatic aberration*. Both defects arise from the fact that the lenses do not bend all light equally. *Spherical aberration*, or *refractive error*, is the slight blurring of the image caused by the fact that not all rays of light come into focus at the same point. Similarly, the different wavelengths of white light are refracted unequally, occasionally causing halos of color, like the bluish haze we see around distant objects. This defect is called *chromatic aberration*.

A third natural defect, *presbyopia* — the inability to focus the eyes clearly on close objects — is an inevitable result of aging. The blind spot on the retina, where the optic nerve begins, could also be called a natural defect, but it does not cause any difficulty because the brain fills this particular gap in our vision with what it assumes we would be seeing there.

Another group of common eye defects arises from variations in the shape of the eyeball, generally hereditary. The normal eyeball is about 1/25 of an inch longer from front to back than it is from side to side or top to bottom. Such a well-proportioned eyeball is called *emmetropic*. Very few eyeballs have perfectly normal dimensions, but the differences are usually so slight that there is no perceptible effect upon vision. The brain makes whatever small adjustments are necessary.

Eyeballs that are significantly longer than they should be cause nearsightedness, or *myopia*, and abnormally short eyeballs cause *hyperopia*, or farsightedness. A third defect belonging to this group, the most common abnormality of all, is *astigmatism*, caused by irregularities in the cornea or the lens or both, resulting in a distorted image cast upon the retina. All of these conditions can be corrected by the use of appropriate eyeglasses or contact lenses.

Less frequent than the defects already mentioned, but by no means rare, is *strabismus*, which involves an imbalance of the six muscles controlling the movements of each eye. (A form of strabismus is also caused by paralysis of one or more of the eye muscles.) The imbalance pulls the eyes out of alignment, causing crossed eyes (*esotropia*), divergent or outward-turning eyes (*exotropia*), or an upward or downward misalignment (*hypertropia* or *hypotropia*).

Strabismus can also create an inability to combine the pictures seen through each eye into a single image. A person so afflicted may see two images, perhaps of two different sizes, and so on. Such disturbances, fortunately rare, may also be the fault of imperfect nerve transmission of the retinal images to the brain, or may even result from errors of interpretation in the cerebral cortex.

When we fail to see things clearly, we may unconsciously tighten or relax the muscles that control the shape of the lens. This is called an *accommodative squint*, since we are attempting to accommodate our vision to the distance of the object.

Finally, there is the condition called *amblyopia*, a dimness or impairment of vision that cannot be attributed to any detectable organic defect, either in the eye itself or in the optic nerve. Some forms of amblyopia are linked to intense emotional disturbances, such as hysteria; to alcoholism; to the toxic effects of arsenic, quinine, and other drugs; to excessive smoking; and even to fatigue.

"Extraordinary" Problems

Glaucoma and cataracts are generally considered the most serious of the "extraordinary" problems. Although it can be controlled, glaucoma is one of the major causes of blindness in the United States, and probably in most of the rest of the world. Yet, with proper care, much of its damage is preventable.

Cataracts also cause blindness in the affected eye. While not preventable, this condition can be corrected to a considerable degree by the removal of the involved lens and the substitution of a contact or other corrective lens.

Besides these two very serious problems there are a number of others that can result in loss or impairment of sight. Various portions of the eye are subject to illness or damage. Some conditions like detached retina, in which the retina comes loose from the choroid against which it normally rests, can be repaired if detected in time. Others, like the retinal damage — retinopathy — that is often seen in diabetes or in high blood pressure, may be extremely difficult to correct. But even in these areas, where the prospect was exceedingly gloomy until recent years, new developments offer considerable hope for improvement.

The eyes are also subject to a series of infections and inflammations, including conjunctivitis, retinitis, uveitis, and papillitis or inflammation of the optic nerve. Various tumors, growths, disturbances of circulation, poisons, and injuries may also threaten our sight, along with hazards from sunlight, ultraviolet, and other radiation, heat, and chemical irritants.

Beyond all these there are a number of degenerative changes, as well as injuries to the brain and other parts of our bodies that can exercise a damaging effect upon our vision. Certain forms of liver disease have been found to produce temporary color blindness; and kidney disease, by interfering with the normal process that purifies the blood, can result in serious eye problems. The blood, after all, provides the eyes as well as the rest of the body with the nutrients and chemicals they need to work properly. If the body's wastes and other toxic materials are not adequately eliminated from the blood, but are instead carried to the eyes, our eyesight is likely to suffer.

Recently, Research to Prevent Blindness, Inc., reported the results of a survey into the causes of blindness in the United States:

Eight out of ten cases of blindness, it was found, result from diseases whose causes are not yet known to science.

Glaucoma, cataract, detached retina, and similar eye diseases of unknown cause are responsible for 38 percent of blindness.

General diseases such as diabetes, hypertension, and other circulatory ills are involved in 16 percent of blindness.

In 14 percent of all cases of blindness, the cause was either unknown or unspecified.

Infectious disease was involved in 10 percent of the nation's blindness.

In 9 percent, the cause was unknown but believed to be prenatal in origin.

Injuries were held responsible in 5 percent; hereditary causes in 4 percent, and poisoning in 3 percent.

In only one case of blindness in every hundred was a neoplastic, or cancerous, growth held responsible.

Considering the complexity of our eyes and measuring this against the countless hazards to which they are exposed each day, it is amazing how little actually does go wrong. With a modicum of good sense, care, caution and proper medical attention, most of the dangers can be kept under adequate control.

EYE CHANGES ASSOCIATED WITH GENERAL DISEASE

Bernard Seeman

MANY DISEASES which affect the entire body frequently are revealed in the eye at an early stage, making possible the diagnosis of a generalized disease process by examining the eyes.

The eye is a window to the vascular system of the body. By using an ophthalmoscope, a physician can visualize the retinal arteries and veins which often manifest changes in the blood vessels throughout the body. Thus the retinal blood vessels of patients with incipient high blood pressure, diabetes, endocrine disorders, or hardening of the arteries will show characteristic changes.

Other systemic diseases will affect the clarity of the lens, the amount of tear formation, the eye muscles, and so on. The ophthalmologist frequently suspects a general disease process and refers a patient to the appropriate physician for diagnostic procedures and treatment.

Arteriosclerosis (hardening of the arteries), the most common change in the arterioles, is associated with the aging process. Arteriosclerotic changes in the eye are primarily limited to the arteries. Most individuals show arteriosclerosis after they reach the age of fifty years. Persons who have hypertension or diabetes, as well as some individuals with no associated disease, develop these changes earlier.

The basic problem in arteriosclerosis is thickening of the walls of the blood vessels, compressing the blood column and making it smaller and smaller. As the sclerosis progresses, the walls of the arteries become hard. It is easy to see the sclerotic walls of the blood vessels with the ophthalmoscope.

Occasionally blood vessels will become plugged. If this happens to the main artery entering through the optic nerve, the entire blood supply to the retina is shut off. This disaster, called *occlu-*

sion of the central retinal artery, results in sudden, almost complete, blindness for which there is no adequate treatment.

If, after it has entered the eye and is coursing over the retina, one of the branches of the central retinal artery becomes occluded, the retinal tissue it supplied will die and cause a partial defect in the field of vision. The defect will correspond to the area of the retina that has been deprived of its blood supply.

A similar sclerotic process can occur in the veins of the retina. When a sclerotic vein becomes totally or partially occluded, the increased pressure caused by the back-up of venous blood behind the area of the occlusion first weakens and then breaks through the wall. Hemorrhage results. *Occlusion of a retinal vein* is usually associated with large retinal hemorrhages which are easily seen with the ophthalmoscope. Occlusion of a retinal artery collapses the vessels behind the clot and, because the wall of an artery is much stronger than the wall of a vein, there is no break. All that the ophthalmoscope shows is pallor and loss of the normal pink color of the blood vessel and retina beyond the area of occlusion.

HYPERTENSION. Persons who have high blood pressure (hypertension) show characteristic changes in their retinal arteries. Spasms or narrowing of the arterial walls are the earliest changes. Perhaps, these changes actually provoke hypertension in some individuals, because it takes a higher pressure to force the same amount of blood through smaller vessels.

The muscular walls of the arterial blood vessels contract, narrowing the vessels and forcing the heart to work harder to push blood at a higher pressure through the narrowed arteries. This so-called *essential hypertension* occurs for no apparent reason. As the arterial spasms continue and sclerotic thickening occurs in the vessel walls, the pressure may become so high that, like an old garden hose, the vessels break and spray red blood around the posterior portion of the eye.

The typical *flame shape* of these hemorrhages results from the distribution of the arterial system in the retina. The retinal arterioles run on the inner surface of the retina. At this level, the nerve fibers course toward the optic nervehead in sheets or bundles. When the blood vessel breaks, the blood fans out along the nerve fibers and causes a hemorrhage that looks exactly like a flame; or as if the retina had received one sideways brush stroke of red paint. In more severe hypertension, the optic nerve may become edematous and surrounded by flame-shaped hemorrhages.

Cotton-wool exudates (discharges) occur here and there in retinas in which the blood supply has been impaired. In such cases, the partially damaged vessel walls leak fluid, but not the larger red blood cells, into the retina.

If severe hypertension lasts long enough, vision can be damaged. These cases are rare, however. Patients with severe hypertensive retinopathy seldom live long.

If hypertension is diagnosed early, it usually can be controlled medically; the retinal changes, if they have not progressed to the severe later stages, are readily reversible. The spastic blood vessels will return to normal size; any small hemorrhages will absorb

2. ETIOLOGY

without damage to the eye; the cotton-wool patches will absorb and the edematous nerve will return to normal.

One severe form of hypertensive retinopathy occurs in pregnant women toward the time of delivery. For no apparent reason, their blood pressure will suddenly shoot with extreme rapidity to a high level. All the changes found in hypertensive retinopathy may occur in just a few days. Simply terminating the pregnancy and delivering the baby, if necessary by Caesarean section, will correct this situation which, fortunately, is rare. When it does occur during pregnancy, it is a serious threat to the mother's life. The condition is called *eclampsia*.

DIABETES MELLITUS. Diabetes is a common disease that is due to numerous complex factors. Simply, the cause is the failure of the pancreas to produce enough insulin to metabolize the blood sugar properly. Eventually diabetes involves blood vessels everywhere in the body, but its most obvious effect is on the eyes and the kidneys.

Diabetic retinopathy seldom occurs in the diabetic patient until the disorder has existed for at least five years. Some patients with a history of diabetes for several decades show absolutely no signs of diabetic retinopathy. It is not unusual for persons who are afflicted with diabetes during childhood or adolescence to manifest more severe forms of diabetic retinopathy during their adulthood than those who developed milder forms of diabetes later in life.

Probably the most characteristic early change in the retinal blood vessels of diabetic patients is a *microaneurysm*. The small ballooning out of the wall of an arteriole, which normally is virtually invisible, becomes visible during an ophthalmoscopic examination. The ophthalmologist can see the dilated sac of pooled blood on the otherwise invisible vessel; to him, the microaneurysm looks like a small cherry or a small cluster of cherries in an apparently avascular portion of the retina. Actually, the dilatation is on the venous side of the capillary network, not on the arterial side. Diabetes generally affects the veins more severely than the arterioles.

After the microaneurysms appear, *hard* discharges that resemble tiny drops of wax are seen here and there on the retinal surface. Next, *blot or dot hemorrhages* become scattered over the retina. These hemorrhages look like blots because they occur in the deeper layers of the retina (in contrast to flame-shaped hypertensive hemorrhages) where the more compact nerve tissue allows the blood to spread only a little.

In the final stages of diabetic retinopathy, enormous retinal and preretinal hemorrhages occur. Hemorrhages into the vitreous make that structure opaque. Often, the retina is not visible; if it is, one will discover the presence of scar formation. Shrinking of the elastic scar tissue pulls on the retinal surface. Eventually, a hole will develop in the retina, and retinal detachment will ensue.

In an attempt to maintain the blood supply to the retina, new blood vessels form, proliferate, and course about the nervehead and out onto the surface of the retina. Since these blood vessels are extremely fragile, they break easily and cause more hemorrhaging which results in additional scar formation and further deterioration inside the eye. At last the retina detaches completely. The eye is blind.

The therapy for diabetic retinopathy is unsatisfactory at best. Many different treatments have been tried. Some physicians feel that maintaining excellent control of the diabetes tends to delay or prevent serious retinal consequences. However, many patients under excellent diabetic control have developed diabetic retinopathy and become blind.

Photocoagulation (burning with light) of the peripheral blood vessels when microaneurysms begin to form occasionally gives satisfactory results. The method has not been used long enough for adequate evaluation of the long-term results.

Any treatment of diabetic retinopathy is very difficult to evaluate because the disease tends to have remissions and exacerbations. Microaneurysms may disappear for no apparent reason. Hemorrhages may disappear spontaneously. The condition may suddenly improve for reasons unknown. On the other hand, an almost normal-appearing diabetic eye may, over a short period, progress through all the stages of diabetic retinopathy.

Cataract formation, as well as diabetic retinopathy, occurs frequently in diabetic patients. Often an opacity forms in the posterior portion of the lens in the very center where it greatly reduces vision. Typical senile cataracts may also appear in diabetic patients, often at an early age.

Paralysis of one or more extraocular muscle is not unusual in diabetics; nor is optic neuritis or optic atrophy. The incidence of these conditions is much higher in diabetic patients than in the general population.

Sudden changes in refraction occur in diabetics. As the blood-sugar level fluctuates so does the refractive status, often as much as several diopters. These changes are due to variations in the hydration of the lens. If any of his patients show frequent fluctuations in refraction, the ophthalmologist suspects the presence of diabetes and recommends that diabetic tests be performed as soon as possible.

THYROTOXICOSIS. Persons who have disturbances of the thyroid gland frequently manifest characteristic eye changes. *Lid lag* is the most common symptom. As the patient looks from up to down, the eyelid, instead of following the downward course in a smooth, normal pattern, tends to remain in the wide-open position for an instant or two. Then, suddenly, almost as if it were just getting the signal, the eyelid will move downward to cover the top of the eye. This immediately suggests the presence of an incipient hyperthyroid problem.

Often, in persons with severe hyperthyroidism, the eyes bulge forward and give a wide-open, fixed gaze appearance. Often, too, these patients develop alterations in their eye movements because of weakness of the eye muscles. Especially affected is convergence. It becomes more and more difficult to focus both eyes on reading material. Double vision and, perhaps, headaches result.

Treatment of hyperthyroidism generally brings about some im-

2. ETIOLOGY

provement in the eye findings. However, especially if the hyperthyroidism is quite severe, the eyes protrude and the protrusion may be permanent. The condition is called *proptosis*.

Protuberant eyes become exposed and dry more rapidly than normal. Any dust or dirt in the air is more likely to fall on the exposed eye. Patients with the proptosis of hyperthyroidism complain of dry, burning, irritated eyes. Frequent use of lubricating eyedrops and eye washes will alleviate the irritation. Occasionally, however, the eyelids must be partially closed by a surgical procedure in order to protect the eyes.

Some common infectious diseases that may involve the eyes are tuberculosis, syphilis, measles, smallpox, herpes simplex and herpes zoster (shingles). Reactions to smallpox vaccine may also involve the eyes.

Tuberculosis most often causes iritis or chorioretinitis. It may also cause scleritis or episcleritis (inflammation of the sclera). Tuberculosis may also affect the ocular blood vessels, causing retinal hemorrhages. Active tuberculosis can migrate into the interior of the eye and produce tuberculous endophthalmitis, disintegrating the entire eye and turning it into a bag of pus.

Syphilis is a much more subtle disease. It may be present congenitally from the mother and result in *Hutchinson's* famous *triad* of saddle nose, deafness and notched incisor teeth, along with interstitial keratitis.

The most common eye lesion in syphilis is interstitial keratitis, a haziness of the deep stromal layers of the cornea. Frequently associated with this form of keratitis are vascularization and low-grade chronic iritis.

Acquired syphilis may cause chorioretinitis and degeneration of the retina, as well as interstitial keratitis, later in life.

Various changes in the way the pupil reacts to light are characteristic of syphilis. Known as the *Argyll Robertson pupil*, the changes assist in diagnosing syphilis.

Herpes simplex is a viral disease manifested most often as a *cold sore* on the lips. However, if a cold sore attacks the cornea, the result is *herpetic keratitis*. This entity is described in the chapter on the cornea.

Herpes zoster (shingles) ophthalmicus is caused by invasion of the shingles virus into the nucleus of the fifth cranial nerve, the nerve that supplies the middle portion of the face from the forehead to the cheek and controls all sensation in the eye, the eyelids and the surrounding tissues. The skin on the involved side of the face breaks down and forms blisters. If the eye becomes involved, keratitis, iritis and, occasionally, optic neuritis occur. In most cases, the condition clears by itself. To protect the eye, such supportive medications as topical antibiotics and corticosteroids may be needed.

If *German measles* (rubella) infects a woman during pregnancy, it generally causes a number of congenital anomalies in the child, including several serious ocular disorders. Cataracts, usually bilateral, are the most common eye abnormality. Rubella-infected children may be born with bilateral cataracts, *nystagmus* (oscillating eyes), *microphthalmos* (extremely small, nonfunctioning eyes), and strabismus.

Cataract surgery should be delayed until the child is at least two years of age. Surgery could activate the live rubella virus still present in the ocular tissues during the child's early life and cause complete loss of the eye.

Measles (rubeola) may produce acute conjunctivitis during its course. Occasionally, keratitis results. A youngster with measles should receive systemic and local antibiotics if conjunctivitis appears.

Smallpox is rare today. If it does occur it can cause considerable damage to the eyes. More frequent is the occurrence of smallpox vesicles on the eyelids or the surface of the eye produced by *smallpox vaccination.* Usually, the infection results from the child rubbing the area of vaccination and then rubbing his eyes. Prevention is, of course, not to touch the vaccination before it is completely healed.

Certain vitamins and drugs can cause ocular complications. *Hypovitamin* A (lack of vitamin A) causes night blindness (xerophthalmia). Vitamin A is essential to the formation of visual purple in the retina, and visual purple is essential to the proper function of the rod cells. If vitamin A levels in the body become extremely low, visual purple will not function properly; the rods will not work, and night blindness will ensue.

Proper metabolism of the cornea also depends on vitamin A. If vitamin A is long absent from the diet, the cornea becomes dry and hazy, and its epithelium will slough off. As corneal sensitivity decreases, the cornea's defense against bacteria lessens. The infected corneal ulcers that appear scar the cornea. Severe visual loss may result.

Fortunately, vitamin A deficiency is seldom seen in the Western World. It is prevalent in the malnourished populations of Asia and Africa.

The obvious treatment for lack of vitamin A is administration of vitamin A, generally intramuscularly at first. If corneal scarring has not occurred, this therapy produces rapid return of normal night vision as well as corneal clearing.

It is also possible to get too much vitamin A. This fat-soluble vitamin cannot be excreted from the body at a rapid rate. If a health faddist takes too much vitamin A, various tissues, such as the skin and the sclera, will turn yellow. Too much vitamin A can also affect the brain, causing bilateral papilledema. Conceivably, such patients could die of brain damage.

Anticholinergics (atropine and related drugs) are given systemically for various gastrointestinal disorders. Ophthalmologists also use these preparations topically to dilate the pupil and paralyze the ciliary body during refraction. In large doses, these drugs paralyze accommodation which causes dilatation of the pupil and blurring of vision. More dangerous, if the patient who takes these drugs has an anterior chamber with a narrow angle, is the possibility of an acute attack of glaucoma. Dilatation of the pupil causes the iris to block the angle and the ocular drainage system.

2. ETIOLOGY

Occasionally, a case of acute glaucoma occurs in hospitals after a patient has been given anticholinergic drugs before general surgery.

ORAL CONTRACEPTIVES. Numerous recent reports suggest that oral contraceptives may precipitate ophthalmic vascular occlusive disease or damage the optic nerve. Occurrences of both of these conditions in patients on oral contraceptives have been documented. So many women take these preparations that it is difficult to establish whether the ocular afflictions are due to the oral contraceptive or whether they would have occurred anyway. At this time, it seems likely that oral contraceptives are safe when taken by normal healthy women with no history of vascular or ocular disease.

Corticosteroids are used widely in medicine both systemically and, in ophthalmology and dermatology, topically. In certain susceptible persons, systemic corticosteroids can cause, over a period of time, increased intraocular pressure, which eventually leads to glaucoma.

Corticosteroids can worsen episodes of fungal keratitis and herpes simplex keratitis. Long-term use of these preparations often stimulates the development of posterior subcapsular cataracts. Usually the cataracts are mild and cause little decrease in vision, but they can be a significant complication of long-term corticosteroid therapy.

Digitalis in high doses may cause blurred vision and disturbed color sensation. Usually, when the digitalis dose is lowered, these symptoms clear. Patients suffering from digitalis intoxication may notice that objects appear yellow or green or, sometimes, snowy white.

OXYGEN. Any high concentration of oxygen may cause transient visual blurring in adults. An occasional patient with inactive retrobulbar neuritis may suffer almost complete loss of the visual field following the administration of oxygen.

The most serious consequence of oxygen administration occurs in premature infants. If they receive high concentrations of oxygen for a prolonged period, *retrolental fibroplasia* may affect the eyes. This tragedy is described in the chapter on the retina.

EYE DISEASES: WHAT CAN BE DONE ABOUT THEM?

BY PHYLLIS LEHMANN

You can get a detached retina as easily at 23 as at 40. And by 30, glaucoma already is a risk. But progress is now being made in preventing and treating serious eye diseases and disorders, to protect the most precious gift we have.

In a world so dependent on the printed word, electronic images, and complex tools, it is not surprising that visual impairment ranks just after heart disease and arthritis among chronic diseases that most severely interfere with a normal life.

The National Eye Institute estimates that nearly four million new cases of eye disease occur each year in the U.S., requiring more than 31 million visits to the doctor.

Some diseases—such as the highly infectious trachoma, which still causes widespread blindness in many parts of the world—have been virtually wiped out in this country. But as life expectancy increases, those associated with aging—cataracts, glaucoma, degeneration of the retina—have become leading causes of blindness.

Fortunately, there are heartening developments in research on the causes, prevention and treatment of eye diseases. As Dr. W. Morton Grant, the David Glendenning Cogan professor of Ophthalmology at Harvard Medical School, points out in *The Horizons of Health* (Harvard University Press), extensive study of the living eye dates back only about 50 years. Yet, thanks to such developments as X-rays, ultrasound and radioisotopes, it is now possible for scientists to investigate what is going on in the diseased eye. Instruments are available for measuring the pressure inside the eye and even inside the blood vessels of the eye. Improved surgical techniques have simplified cataract operations and are restoring vision in once hopeless cases of retinal disorders. Scientists are on the threshold of discovering the biochemical causes of such disorders as glaucoma and those associated with diabetes.

DISEASES OF THE RETINA AND CHOROID

Diseases of the retina, the light-sensitive tissue at the back of the eye, and the choroid, an underlying layer rich in blood vessels that help nourish the retina, are responsible for more cases of blindness in this country than any other eye disorders.

For a number of the disorders there is no known cure or means of prevention. But through medical and surgical improvements, doctors can preserve or restore vision for many victims. Retinal and choroid diseases include:

Diabetic retinopathy. Before the advent of insulin in 1921, few diabetics lived long enough to develop eye complications. Today diabetic retinopathy threatens the vision of more than 300,000 people each year and is responsible for about 10 per cent of all new cases of blindness. Among those aged 45 to 74, it accounts for 20 per cent of all loss of sight and is the leading cause of all newly reported blindness between the ages of 24 to 64.

In some way that is still a mystery to scientists, diabetes causes the blood vessel system in the retina to go awry. In the severe form of the disease, abnormal blood vessels grow on the surface of the retina and often protrude into the center of the eye, where they may hemorrhage into the vitreous—the clear gel that fills the eye and keeps it from collapsing like a deflated balloon. When the blood-filled vitreous prevents light from reaching the retina, vision is impaired.

Two exciting new techniques, photocoagulation and vitrectomy, are helping to lower the rate of blindness from diabetic retinopathy. An NEI study of more than 1,720 patients at 16 medical centers nationwide has shown that photocoagulation (the use of a laser or xenon arc beam to destroy abnormal blood vessels and diseased retinal tissue) can reduce the risk of blindness from this disease by more than 60 per cent.

Macular degeneration. The macula, a tiny area in the center of the retina that gives us sharp color vision and the ability to read and see fine detail, is especially prone to deterioration. Macular degeneration caused by aging is the leading cause of newly reported blindness over age 64. Many other victims, still able to walk around unaided, have trouble reading signs and recognizing faces.

Scientists suspect that macular degeneration is caused by a breakdown in the supply of blood to the retina, but the disease remains largely a mystery. Once a person goes blind, vision often cannot be restored. Such new techniques as fluorescein angiography, in which a fluorescent dye is injected into the blood stream and its passage through the retinal vessels photographed, make it easier for specialists to pinpoint the type and location of macular disorders.

Uveitis. This term refers to a whole family of diseases that cause inflammation of the uveal tract—the choroid, iris, and ciliary body (the tissue that secretes the aqueous fluid that flows through the front part of the eye and which controls the focusing of the lens). Symptoms range from pain, redness, and hypersensitivity to light in acute cases, to slightly veiled vision or floating spots—probably caused by inflamed cells in the vitreous—in chronic cases. Uveitis can be detected in a routine eye examination. Untreated, it can lead to other eye diseases, such as glaucoma.

For the most part, causes of uveitis remain unknown. Some research indicates that prostaglandins, a group of substances commonly released by the body after cell injury, appear within the eye in certain types of uveitis, and may contribute to the inflammation. Scientists now are testing drugs that counteract the prostaglandins. Currently, cortisone is the most popular and effective treatment for uveitis.

Retinitis pigmentosa. There is no known treatment to prevent a person who carries the gene for retinitis pigmentosa from gradually losing night vision and side vision. The first symptom generally is loss of night vision, which shows up in childhood or adolescence. Fortunately, not all victims go blind. Many even retain their reading vision, although it may be severely limited to a small central field.

Retinitis pigmentosa gets its name from unusual deposits of black pigment scattered through the retina and especially around the edges. Considerable

> **Next to the brain, the eye is the most complex organ in the human body.**

2. ETIOLOGY

progress is being made in understanding the possible causes of the disease. It is now believed to result from changes in the pigmented layer of the retina which plays an important role in the normal growth and renewal of the light-sensitive retinal cells.

Detached retina. This is one retinal disorder that lends itself readily to surgical repair if detected early enough. When a tear or hole develops in the retina, fluid from the vitreous can seep between the inner and outer layers of the retina and cause them to separate. If they separate completely, blindness results.

A common symptom is the feeling that a curtain has been drawn across the eyes. Seeing sootlike spots or flashes of light can indicate tears in the retina or a problem in the vitreous that may lead to retinal detachment. Before actual detachment occurs, tears or holes in the retina can sometimes be sealed by beams of intense light (photocoagulation) or by extreme cold (cryosurgery).

If a detached retina is diagnosed early, the separated layers can be reattached in 85 per cent of cases and vision often restored.

Often, vitreous lost through the detached layers of the retina is replaced during surgery by a salt solution, which helps keep the layers in place and maintains the shape of the eye. Under investigation for holding badly detached retinal layers in place is a gas, sulfur hexafluoride, which has the unusual property of swelling when it is injected into the eye.

● GLAUCOMA

More than one million Americans, the majority of them over 35, suffer from glaucoma. Though treatable if diagnosed early, the disease remains a leading cause of blindness.

In the normal eye, a fluid known as aqueous humor, secreted into the eye to nourish the cornea and lens, can pass out into the bloodstream through a system of tiny drainage channels. In glaucoma, this filtration area becomes blocked. The aqueous humor builds up, causing increased pressure that eventually damages the optic nerve.

Glaucoma is most common among people with a family history of the disease. It can be detected by a simple procedure known as tonometry, which measures pressure within the eye. This test should be performed regularly every year, especially after age 30, and if there is a family history of the disease.

An attack of acute glaucoma can cause blurred vision, an illusion of colored halos around lights, enlarged pupils, and pain. Because the pain can produce severe nausea and vomiting, acute glaucoma is frequently misdiagnosed in hospital emergency rooms as an abdominal condition. Anyone who suffers this combination of symptoms should seek immediate medical attention.

There are two common types of chronic glaucoma: open-angle, in which the space, or angle, between the iris and the drainage channels is open but the drains themselves are obstructed and acute angle-closure, in which the angle is unusually narrow and may become suddenly blocked if the iris should be pushed forward. Often there are no obvious symptoms of the more common open-angle type, and the disease can advance to a severe state before the victim is even aware of it. Once the optical nerve has been damaged, however, reversal of the damage is impossible.

The angle-closure type can give some advance warning in the form of pain, blurred vision, or a halo effect. One method of treating it is to remove a piece of the iris.

If detected early by examination, open-angle glaucoma can usually be successfully controlled, but not cured, with drugs. The most common, pilocarpine, is now available in the form of a wafer that is inserted under the eyelid about once a week. For young people and those with mild cases of glaucoma, this is more convenient than applying drops several times a day.

Because pilocarpine constricts the pupil, allowing less light into the eye, the patient experiences dimmed vision, especially when inside a building or during evening hours. Timolol, a new drug still under investigation, shows promise for lowering pressure within the eye without producing this unpleasant side effect.

Several exciting lines of research may lead eventually to prevention of glaucoma. Scientists have noted, for example, that long-term use of cortisone and related drugs to treat eye inflammations causes increased eye pressure in some people, particularly those who have a family history of glaucoma. This discovery opens up the possibility of a blood test to identify very early those most likely to develop the disease.

Dr. Grant reports that a great deal of attention is now centering on the optic nerve and how it is damaged by glaucoma. Some people are able to withstand eye pressure without any harm to the optic nerve while others go blind from just a slight increase in pressure. The ultimate goal of research in this area, Dr. Grant says, is to find some way of treating weak optic nerves to make them better able to withstand pressure. Most present treatment is aimed at reducing the pressure.

● CATARACT

Contrary to popular belief, a cataract is *not* a film or membrane that grows over the eye. It is a cloudiness or opacity in the lens—the normally clear portion of the eye between the iris and the vitreous that helps focus images on the retina. When the lens is clouded, light has trouble getting through to the retina, and vision is impaired.

Typically, a person who develops cataract in one eye will develop it in the other. Common symptoms of the disease are hazy vision, double vision in one eye, and a dazzling sensation while driving at night, because the clouded lens scatters light from the headlights of approaching cars.

No one knows for certain what causes cataract. The most common form, known as senile cataract, is associated with normal aging of the eye and afflicts more than two million Americans over age 65. Recent studies at Columbia University and the Massachusetts Institute of Technology indicate that clumping of protein within the lens reduces transparency. Researchers suspect that high concentrations of calcium may be responsible for the protein clumps. If their theory proves accurate, it may be possible to develop drugs that would inhibit the clumping process and delay the formation of cataracts.

Another form of cataract is sugar cataract, which occurs in diabetics. Sugars in the lens are metabolized to sugar alcohols; these accumulate in the lens and cause it to swell and cloud. Scientists have recently developed an experimental

drug that slows down the formation of sugar alcohols in animals. The next step is a drug that works safely and effectively in humans. The sugar cataract is rare in humans; most likely, the process may help accelerate the formation of senile cataracts in diabetics. More important is the fact that the same basic process which causes sugar cataracts to form may cause early damage to blood vessels in diabetic retinopathy and in other vascular complications of the disease. Thus an inhibitory drug may be more useful in preventing these complications than for the sugar cataracts themselves.

For now, surgery is the only treatment for cataract. The most common operation is complete removal of the clouded lens. Modern refinements in cataract surgery include introducing an enzyme to weaken the ligaments that hold the lens in place and using an extremely cold probe which freezes to the lens so that it can be lifted easily from the eye.

A recently developed method of removing cataracts is phacoemulsification, in which the surgeon pulverizes the lens with high-frequency sound waves and draws out the fragments through a hollow needle.

To replace the natural lens, cataract patients may be fitted with thick lenses that magnify 20 to 35 per cent. The glasses produce distortion and limit side vision. Contact lenses are an alternative and give better sight, but many elderly patients do not have the dexterity to handle them. The intraocular lens, a tiny plastic device inserted into the eye during surgery, enables a person to see almost normally, but this technique is suited only to a minority of patients.

● CORNEAL DISEASE

Because it is exposed, the outer portion of the eye is susceptible to all sorts of bacterial, fungus, and viral infections and to allergic reactions. Of all these, diseases that afflict the cornea are the most serious. Because it is packed with nerves, so it can detect if something is on the surface of the eye, corneal disorders are also the most painful of all eye problems. If the cornea becomes clouded or scarred from untreated disease or injury—or despite treatment—the patient can go blind or suffer impaired vision.

The most serious and most common corneal diseases are viral infections which, unlike bacterial infections, often resist drug treatment. The most prevalent is caused by the herpes simplex virus, the one responsible for cold sores. Because the virus lodges in the nerves at the back of the eye, infection often recurs.

A major breakthrough in combating herpes simplex came in the 1960s with discovery of idoxuridine (IDU), the first drug used successfully to treat a human virus infection. A new drug, vidarabine, which is just as effective as IDU but without some of the unpleasant side effects, has just been put on the market. Although these drugs alleviate the symptoms of herpes simplex infections, no drug has yet been found that will actually kill the persistent virus.

Some of the discomfort of corneal disease can be alleviated by the new, fluid-filled soft contact lenses, which are now widely used as "bandages" to prevent the eyelid from rubbing against a tender cornea.

For those who do go blind from corneal disease, transplants offer a second chance for normal eyesight. They are the most successful of all human transplants because the absence of blood vessels in the cornea reduces the danger of tissue rejection.

A recent major advance in cornea transplants was the development by University of Florida scientists of a new tissue culture solution in which fresh corneas can be kept for up to a week with no special handling. Previously, many cornea transplants had to be done on almost an emergency basis, because fresh corneas begin to deteriorate after 48 hours, even under refrigeration.

● SENSORY-MOTOR DISORDERS

Probably less is known about this category of diseases—which involve the nerves or muscles of the eye or interfere with the transmission of visual information to the brain—than about any other eye disorders. The NEI estimates that 31,500 people in this country are blind because of atrophy, or wasting away, of the optic nerve. The most common types of sensory-motor disorders include strabismus and amblyopia, two conditions which occur in early childhood and should be corrected as soon as possible.

● WILL THERE EVER BE AN EYE TRANSPLANT?

Looking far into the future, one question in eye research is whether doctors will ever be able to transplant a working eye from one human being to another or implant an artificial eye that will work like a natural one. For the time being such feats belong to science fiction. Next to the brain, the eye is the most complex organ in the human body and, in fact, could be considered an extension of the brain. The optic nerve alone has 150 million fibers to carry messages to the brain. But in an age when tiny beams of light can repair damage deep within the eye and when parts of the eye can be replaced by pieces of plastic or a salt solution, nothing can be considered permanently impossible.

INJURIES

Bernard Seeman

INJURIES TO the eyes are common even with the extensive use of industrial safety goggles and widespread publicity emphasizing protection of the eyes. A corneal *foreign body* or speck in the eye is the most common eye injury. A small piece of a foreign substance, a cinder, perhaps, becomes imbedded in the cornea or in the conjunctiva of the upper or lower eyelid, causing a scratchy sensation and irritation.

Usually, a foreign body can be removed from the conjunctiva with a cotton applicator without the help of a physician. If the foreign body is imbedded in the corneal epithelium or in deeper corneal tissues, local anesthesia (instillation of a drop of Opthane® or tetracaine) is required before the foreign body can be easily removed with a sharp, knifelike instrument called a corneal spud. After removal of the foreign body, the small pit or crater in the corneal surface will be closed rapidly by the surrounding epithelium growing into the area of the defect.

To promote rapid healing, antibiotic eyedrops and a patch should be applied to the eye. The eye patch will immobilize the eyelids and decrease the friction between the eyelids and the epithelial surface, allowing the epithelium to grow more rapidly.

A corneal abrasion caused by a foreign body will usually heal within twenty-four hours. When a twig, a fingernail, or some other object scratches the surface of the cornea, a corneal abrasion results. It, too, will heal rapidly if an antibiotic solution is instilled and the eye is patched.

Occasionally, however, linear corneal abrasions recur weeks or months after healing of the original injury. Indeed, there may be several recurrences over a period of years. The probable cause is failure of the epithelial cells to become adequately reattached to the underlying Bowman's membrane during the initial healing. A foreign body sensation and discomfort warn of the recurrence. Treatment consists of repatching the eye and allowing the abrasion to reheal.

Actinic or ultraviolet radiation keratitis is another type of injury that can cause damage to the corneal epithelium. It is due to prolonged exposure to a sun lamp or to the direct rays of the sun. The actinic radiation causes the epithelium to break down, usually within six to twelve hours after exposure to the ultraviolet light. Many dotlike spots cover the corneal surface after it is stained with fluorescein. The involved areas have a punctate, moth-eaten appearance. To the observing ophthalmologist, the cornea looks as if it had been peppered with microscopic buckshot.

An ultraviolet burn is treated with antibiotic eyedrops and the eye is patched for twenty-four to forty-eight hours. Although actinic keratitis is very uncomfortable, it seldom causes permanent damage to the eye.

Flash burns of the eye resemble ultraviolet keratitis. *Chemical burns* of the eye can be extremely serious. Lye causes the most dangerous of ocular chemical burns because its progressive chemical reaction first destroys the protein of the corneal epithelium, then of Bowman's membrane and, finally, the corneal stroma. Lye burns are frequently bilateral and often result in extreme scarring of both corneas and of the conjunctiva. Shrinkage of the conjunctiva causes the eyelashes to roll in and further irritate the surface of the eye. Eyes burned with lye are difficult to graft (corneal transplant) successfully.

Treatment of lye burns is usually symptomatic. There is, however, a new chemical preparation which seems to reduce the amount of reaction in the corneal epithelium, as well as the amount of scar formation.

Any potent industrial chemical (acids, alkalis, strong salt solutions, cleaning compounds) can also cause chemical burns of the eyes.

Water is the best and most important prophylactic treatment for any ocular chemical burn. As soon as the chemical comes in contact with the eye, the eye should be immediately, vigorously and copiously irrigated with water. Anyone who gets a chemical in his eye should put his head under the nearest faucet, turn on the water and let it run over the eye for five to ten minutes. Any of the chemical removed immediately will not damage the eye; any that is allowed to remain will cause prolonged and extensive damage.

Many foreign bodies of the eye remain in the superficial cornea. A foreign body from a rapidly moving object (a piece of drill bit, bb pellets, the end of a stick or dart) can penetrate the cornea or sclera and become lodged in the interior of the eye, usually the vitreous.

An occasional foreign body travels directly through the eye, penetrating the cornea or sclera on its way in, penetrating the sclera at the back of the eye, and finally, lodging in the orbit or the bony wall of the orbit. If the foreign body remains lodged in the eye, the ophthalmologist must attempt to remove it. Only an inert object (for example, glass) can occasionally be left in the eye without causing further damage.

If the foreign body is magnetic, a magnet can often be used to pull it through an incision in the sclera, choroid and retina. The retina surrounding the incision is cauterized so that detachment will not occur. A nonmagnetic foreign body is difficult to remove. Sometimes, a foreign body in the anterior portion of the eye can be removed by opening the anterior chamber and extracting the object under direct visualization. However, if a nonmagnetic foreign body is in the back of the eye and cannot be directly visualized, successful removal may damage the eye itself.

Penetrating foreign bodies are extremely serious. Frequently, they cause secondary damage to the eye, such as cataract, glaucoma, retinal detachment, and disastrous intraocular infection.

When the surface of the eye is cut through and through by some sharp instrument or tool (a knife, an arrow, a screwdriver) the injury is called *laceration of the globe*. Lacerations usually occur in the cornea. If the lacerations involve the central cornea, the resulting scar will cause considerable loss of vision. Eventually, in these cases, a corneal transplant may successfully restore vision. Secondary complications often follow lacerations of the globe. Cataract and retinal detachment are among the complications.

Any individual with a lacerated globe or a penetrating foreign body in the eye should see an ophthalmologist immediately. In the meantime, the eye should be patched. To prevent further damage, the eye should never be touched or examined by anyone other than an ophthalmologist.

A blunt blow to the eye seldom ruptures the globe. It does, however, cause contusion of the globe which resembles a bruise elsewhere in the body. The blow may produce a shock wave that passes across the contents of the eye and causes damage to the retina. If retinal hemorrhages and edema in the macular area follow the injury, there may be rapid loss of vision. Retinal hemorrhage and macular edema that are not severe usually clear and the patient's vision improves considerably.

Occasionally, blunt trauma to the eye breaks a blood vessel in the iris. The resulting bleeding into the anterior chamber is called *hyphema*. Hyphema is treated by rest to prevent further hemorrhaging. In these cases, it is essential to prevent a rise in the intraocular pressure while the clot occupies the anterior chamber and blocks the trabecular meshwork at the angle. This is a type of glaucoma, which may force the iron pigment from the blood into the cornea, resulting in a tattooed cornea.

If the eye is struck vigorously with a blunt object (for example, a human fist), the floor of the orbit, which is composed of extremely thin bone, will break. This injury, called a *blowout fracture*, may occur concurrently with contusion of the globe, or it may occur when the globe is only slightly injured. A blowout fracture displaces the contents of the orbit through the orbital floor and into the maxillary sinus which lies directly below. If the displacement includes the inferior rectus muscle or the inferior oblique muscle, motion of the eye is limited and pain accompanies each movement. In addition, the eye may have an obvious sunken appearance and lack the prominence of the fellow eye.

To repair the defect in the floor of the orbit, a plastic plate is used to return the contents of the orbit to their rightful position.

VISUAL PIGMENTS AND COLOR BLINDNESS

Color vision depends on three types of cone cell, each containing one of three visual pigments. Those who are color-blind either lack one of the pigments or have an anomalous pigment in one type of cone

by W. A. H. Rushton

"See that little boy; he's blind. Let's put some obstacle in his way and watch him stumble over it." It is almost unthinkable that anyone would play such a trick on a blind person, yet much the same is often done to people who are color-blind. "This little boy is color-blind. Let's ask him the color of these objects and enjoy his confusion when he names the green one red." I mention this because I have been told by my friends, the color-anomalous subjects of my experiments, how they were teased at school and how glad they are to cooperate in a scientific study in which their abnormality is not a joke but a precious pathway to a better understanding not only of abnormal color vision but also of normal color vision.

People with defective color vision can nearly always see a range of colors, particularly along the yellow-blue axis. Thus they tend to resent the implication that they are somehow blind. Their deficiency almost always shows up as abnormal red-green discrimination. The condition is a sex-linked recessive genetic character; therefore the defect is much rarer in women, who have two gene-bearing sex chromosomes (the X chromosomes), than it is in men, who have no second chance if they lack the necessary gene on their single X chromosome. Among men 8 percent have defective red-green vision; among women only .4 percent show the defect.

Two types of red-green defective are recognized, both of which are further subdivided. One type, Type A, consists of dichromats who can match any spectral color by a suitable mixture of lights of two colors, for example red plus blue (without the need for green, which normal eyes require). Such dichromats are monochromatic in the red-green band of the spectrum; hence they can match any wavelength there (that is, in the band between 540 and 700 nanometers) with any other by adjusting only the relative brightness.

Dichromats are divided into two classes: A_1, called protanopes, and A_2, called deuteranopes. Both will say that any wavelength from the red part of the spectrum will match a given green, but protanopes require that the red light be about 10 times brighter than the red selected by the deuteranopes to make the match [see top and middle illustrations on opposite page].

The other type of red-green defective, Type B, is the anomalous trichromat. Defectives of this type resemble normal people in needing three colors (for example red, green and blue) to match all spectral colors, but they insist on abnormal proportions of red and green in their mixtures. They fall into two classes according to the proportions of red and green in the mixture that they match with yellow. Protanomalous trichromats (Type B_1) introduce too much red by normal standards; deuteranomalous trichromats (Type B_2) introduce too much green [see bottom illustration on opposite page].

The anomalous trichromats are not just different from normals; they are indeed somewhat defective. They cannot distinguish nearly as many hues in the spectrum as normals can, and they are confused by autumn tints: the browns and olive greens. Our experiments have shown that in all these defective conditions what is abnormal is one of the photosensitive pigments in the cone cells of the retina. By means of special techniques, which I shall describe, we have been able to measure the spectral sensitivity in the red-green range of each cone pigment in normal eyes and in the eyes of subjects with various color defects.

Since antiquity it has been known that paints can be mixed to obtain new colors. By the 18th century it was generally accepted that there are three primary colors and that all others can be created by mixing them in various ways. In 1802 the English physician Thomas Young located the three primary "colors" not in the physics of light or in the nature of paints but in the color-sensitive mechanisms of the eye. Since Young feared that his patients would lose confidence in him if his addiction to science were known, he wrote very little about his trichromatic theory. Those who assume that what a man has not explicitly stated he has not perceived suppose Young did not see very far.

This ungenerous attitude was not adopted by Hermann von Helmholtz or James Clerk Maxwell, who independently assumed that Young had seen the full implications of his theory. Both made a point of naming him the originator of the three-vector analysis of color vision, which they proceeded to work out. Young had postulated the existence of three resonators in the eye capable of responding maximally to red, yellow (green in a later statement) or blue light. He had concluded that the sensation of color depends on the relative amplitudes of the vibrations induced in the three resonators.

Light, we now know, acts on the photoreceptors of the retina, which are the rods and the cones. The rods are responsible for twilight vision, which is colorless; the cones are responsible for the colored vision of daylight. Toward the end of the 19th century Willy Kühne of Heidelberg discovered the photochemical basis of rod vision. He dissected out frog retinas in the faint yellow light from the flame of a wick steeped with salt and found that the pink retina thus obtained was bleached to a pale yellow on exposure to daylight. This pink pho-

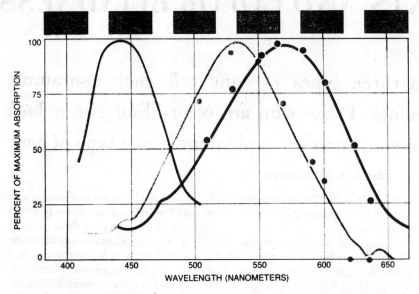

THREE CONE PIGMENTS of normal color vision absorb lights of different wavelengths as plotted here. The curves are the average spectral absorbance from single cones in excised eyes of humans or monkeys scaled to the same maximums. The measurements were made by Edward F. MacNichol, Jr., and his colleagues at Johns Hopkins University. The colored dots represent the pigments in the green-sensitive and red-sensitive cones as they were measured in the living human eye by H. D. Baker and the author at the University of Cambridge. The coincidence of the two sets of measurements demonstrates that single cones contain single pigments. The color patches that appear above the curves approximate the colors of the spectrum at the wavelengths indicated at the bottom of illustration.

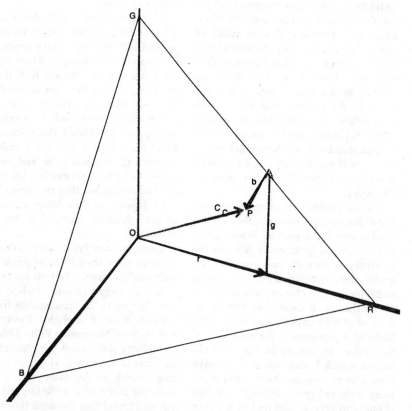

CONCEPT OF "COLOR TRIANGLE" is based on theory of three-pigment color vision. Any given spectral color P (*in this example a pale yellow-orange*) can be matched by a mixture of lights consisting of r units of red, g units of green and b units of blue. The vector sum of r, g and b is the three-dimensional vector OP, the length of which represents brightness. The location C, where arrow OP pierces the color triangle RGB, represents hue.

tosensitive pigment he named rhodopsin. Observing the retina under the microscope, he saw that the pigment was contained in the outer segments of the rods.

Since rhodopsin is bleached by light, it is natural to suppose the change is the basis of rod vision. If that is true, a critical relation must follow: if lights of different wavelengths are adjusted in intensity to look identically bright by the colorless rod vision, they should all bleach rhodopsin at the same rate. This was shown to be the case by German investigators in the 19th century and has been confirmed by more accurate methods since.

By analogy it seemed likely that cones must also contain a photosensitive pigment, different from rhodopsin because the spectral sensitivity of the eye in daylight is not the same as it is in twilight. And presumably in man there are three kinds of cone, each with its own pigment to account for the trichromacy of normal color vision. How are these three cone pigments related to Young's resonators? Young knew the approximate velocity of light from the measurements of Olaus Roemer in 1675, which were confirmed by James Bradley in 1728. Young also inferred the wavelength of light in his own studies of interference fringes, from which he concluded that the resonators vibrate at nearly 10^{15} times per second. No gross object can vibrate as fast as that. What is thrown into oscillation must be something within the "atoms" that John Dalton had just postulated to account for chemical change. We now know that the resonators are electrons, in particular the pi orbitals of molecules, and that their resonance to light at different frequencies is expressed by the pigment's absorbance spectrum.

Young's idea that color results from the independent excitation of three kinds of cone lends itself to a three-vector graphical representation. Three axes mutually at right angles represent the magnitude of excitation of Young's three resonators, or the pigments in the three kinds of cone [*see bottom illustration at left*]. The color represented by a particular point (P) is the vector sum of an excitation (r) of the red-sensitive cones, together with the excitation (g) of green-sensitive cones and the excitation (b) of blue-sensitive cones. If all three components are increased in equal proportions (that is, if the intensity of light P is increased without changing its spectral composition), the result is an increase in the brightness of the mixture without change of color. Therefore the length of the radius vector *OP* signifies brightness, whereas the direction of *OP* signifies color, or hue.

If we imagine a diagonal plane intercepting the three axes at points *R, G* and *B*, we obtain a triangle (the "color triangle"), which is pierced by vectors *OP* representing every possible color; each vector will pierce the triangle at a different point. Many different color triangles have been proposed, depending on the meaning chosen for the term "cone excitation." They are all linear transformations (projections) of one another. Maxwell, who made the first color triangle, chose the most straightforward physically: the vectors of any color *P* were the intensities of three primary lights, a red, a green and a blue whose mixture matched *P*. Intensity units were chosen so that mixing one of each produced white. Thus white was at the center of the triangle.

A more physiological set of vectors is the relative quantum catch (the relative number of photons actually caught) in each of the three types of cone, since this is the immediate precursor of nerve excitation. Such a cone-pigment triangle is shown at the right. The measurement of the quantum catch in each cone pigment, however, is too difficult and imprecise to commend itself to such a meticulous body as the International Commission on Illumination (CIE). The CIE color triangle (like the square root of −1 in alternating-current theory) gives neat and exact answers to calculations by introducing a nearly incomprehensible concept of what is really going on.

If we knew the spectral-absorbance curve for each cone pigment (that is, the spectral sensitivity of each cone), we should be able to calculate the relative quantum catch for any known light. We could then say, for instance, what quantities of red, green and blue Maxwell needed in his mixture to match any spectral light *P*. In other words, we could establish the condition where the quantum catch in each cone is the same from *P* as it is from the mixtures of *R* plus *G* plus *B*.

One might have hoped that the converse would hold, so that from knowing the quantities in the mixture that matches each spectral light we could deduce the spectral sensitivity of each cone. Unfortunately this is not the case. It would be if the red primary light excited only the red-sensitive cones, the green primary excited only the green-sensitive cones and the blue primary excited only the blue-sensitive cones. This, however, is not true. Until we know how much each primary light excites each of

the three kinds of cones, we can say only that the color-mixture functions provide not the three spectral-sensitivity curves but weighted means of those curves, the weighting coefficients being unknown. The most insightful way out of this difficulty was a suggestion made by Arthur Koenig of Berlin at the end of the 19th century.

Koenig recognized that the principal difference between normal vision and the color-defective vision of the dichromat is that to match any wavelength in the red-green spectral range (between 540 and 700 nanometers) the normal person needs two knobs on the color-mixing box, one to regulate the red intensity in the mixture and one to regulate the green, whereas the dichromat, who cannot distinguish red from green, needs only one knob. It makes no difference whether the knob controls a red light or a green one (as perceived by normal people); the dichromat can match any mixture of red and green simply by turning the one knob to achieve matching brightness. Koenig saw that this is

exactly what would follow if the dichromats had only one kind of cone instead of the normal two kinds active in the red-green range: two cones, two dimensions of color, two knobs; one cone, one dimension, one knob.

Two expectations follow and both are true. The first is that there should be two types of red-green confusers, those lacking the red-sensitive cones and those lacking the green. As we have seen, there are indeed two types of dichromats: protanopes, to whom red lights are dim, and deuteranopes, to whom the same lights seem bright. The second expectation is that both types should accept all color matches made by normal eyes. When a person with normal vision matches two fields of color, the red-sensitive pigment catches quanta as fast from the one field as it does from the other, and the green-sensitive pigment does the same. Thus a subject who has only one of these normal pigments will also catch light quanta equally from the two fields and say that they match. This too is found to be true.

In spite of its seductive simplicity, Koenig's theory is not the only one that

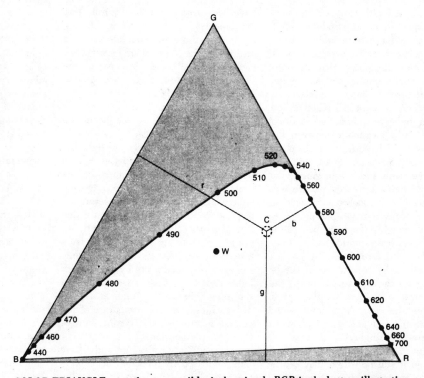

COLOR TRIANGLE, one of many possible, is the triangle *RGB* in the bottom illustration on the opposite page. Perpendiculars *r, g, b* from *C* to the opposite sides *R, G, B* are proportional to *r, g, b* in the preceding illustration. Their lengths correspond to the "quantum catch" (the actual number of photons caught) in *R, G* and *B* cones respectively, each expressed as the fraction of the catch from white light, point *W* in the center of the triangle. The curve shows the position of various monochromatic lights. Note that wavelengths greater than 540 nanometers are not absorbed by blue-sensitive cones. Lights between 510 and 480 nanometers, on the other hand, have appreciable perpendiculars onto all sides of the triangle. Thus these lights are absorbed by all cones, and white appears as a diluent in the resulting sensation. This effect may be reduced by previous adaptation to strong red light.

2. ETIOLOGY

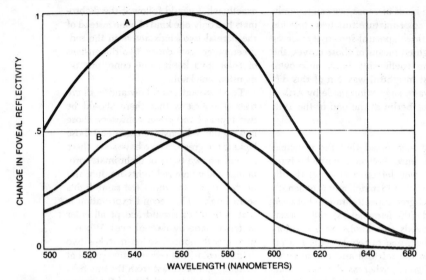

DIFFERENCE SPECTRA of green- and red-sensitive pigments in the normal eye can be determined by shining lights into the eye and measuring the fraction reflected from the foveal region in the center of the retina. Curve A is the change in reflectivity at various wavelengths when a normal dark-adapted fovea is bleached by a strong white light. Curve C is the change from dark adaptation when the bleaching light is a red of a strength sufficient to make the peak of C half the height of the peak of A. Curve B is the change when bleaching light is a bluish green of a strength sufficient to make the peak of B also half that of A.

could account for these facts. An alternative explanation proposed by Adolf Fick of Kassel has been widely entertained, particularly to explain deuteranopia. Fick suggested that deuteranopes have the normal red and green cones but their messages are mixed, so that the brain cannot tell whether red or green light provoked the resulting sensation. The distinction between the Koenig and Fick hypotheses can be paraphrased as follows. An artist with one pot of red paint and one of green who intends to paint a colored picture will be reduced to monochromacy if some prankster either removes one pot (Koenig) or thoroughly mixes the two paints together and leaves nothing but a mustard-colored mixture (Fick). For the Fick hypothesis to be true it would not be necessary for the messages from red and green cones to be mixed on the way to the brain; the equivalent result would obtain if the red and green pigments were mixed in a single class of cones.

Koenig's theory rests on two assumptions, and it will be true if they can be shown to be true: (1) In protanopes and deuteranopes one pigment is absent. (2) The remaining pigments are normal. We have obtained some good evidence to establish the truth of both of these assumptions, as I shall now relate. In order to learn if a subject has one cone pigment or more in the red-green range one would like to be able to measure the pigments objectively. My colleagues and I

have been able to do this by reflection densitometry, which involves shining lights into the living human eye and measuring the amount reflected back [see "Visual Pigments in Man," by W. A. H. Rushton; SCIENTIFIC AMERICAN, November, 1962].

When a cat's eye is caught in the headlights of a car, it is seen to shine back green. Clearly the light has gone into the eye and undergone some selective absorption. By comparing the composition of ingoing and returning light we can measure the spectral absorption. Much of the absorption is due to factors other than visual pigments, but visual pigments are distinguished from everything else by the fact that they alone are bleached away by exposure to light. Thus if we analyze not simply the returning light but its change as a result of bleaching, we have a measure of the change in amount and composition of the visual pigments involved.

Since 1952 my colleagues and I have built and used six reflection densitometers. We have found, contrary to the general expectation, that the pigments in the cones are dense enough for satisfactory measurement. This has encouraged many people to engage in excellent densitometry studies both in intact eyes and in excised retinas. The surprising success of reflection densitometry in measuring cone pigments in the living human eye is mainly due to two anatom-

ical features evolved by nature to perfect our cone vision and now used backward, as it were, to analyze it.

The first feature is that the fovea centralis, the tiny central retinal region of sharpest vision, is devoid of rods, the containers of the pigment rhodopsin, which elsewhere outnumber cones by 100 to one. By confining our densitometry to the fovea we can entirely exclude the overwhelming rhodopsin contribution to the pigments measured. The second helpful feature is that light falling on the retina enters the base of the cones and is focused onto the fine tip where the pigment is, in the same way that a burning glass focuses sunlight. This makes, of course, for an efficient use of the incident light. If one looks through a burning glass at the little area charred, however, one sees the tiny area greatly magnified. In similar fashion the speck of pigment at the tip of each cone is magnified to fill the base, so that the entire foveal floor is virtually filled with cone pigment.

We need not consider here the construction and use of our densitometers. Suffice it to say that the spectral reflectivity of the eye is measured by sending in lights of various wavelengths but of an intensity always too weak to bleach the pigments appreciably. The reflected light is measured by a photomultiplier cell. Bleaching is produced by lights of adjustable wavelength and strength, applied in pulses that alternate with the pulses of measuring light. In this way the change in pigment level can be followed at any wavelength throughout the course of any sequence of bleaching and regeneration.

Now let us see how the densitometer can be used to determine what it is that protanopes and deuteranopes lack. Is it a cone pigment or something in nerve organization? Densitometry measures pigments, not nerves. If nerves are the only thing wrong with dichromats, the densitometer will not be able to detect any abnormality. The fact is that in the normal fovea the densitometer detects two cone pigments (in the red-green range), but in the fovea of a dichromat it detects only one. Hence we can say with confidence that these defectives lack one kind of cone pigment, as Koenig maintained. (This was established some years ago in our work at the University of Cambridge.)

The way to detect two pigments in the normal eye is first to measure the foveal reflectivity with lights of different wavelengths in the unbleached eye. One then exposes the eye to a white light so strong that all pigments are bleached away.

The change of pigment density (not simply the pigment density itself) that is measured at various wavelengths after full bleaching yields a bell-shaped curve with a maximum at about 550 nanometers called the difference spectrum [*curve A in illustration on opposite page*]. The subject is then kept in total darkness for seven minutes to allow his cone pigments to regenerate fully. We now bleach the pigments with a red light of a strength such that the change in pigment density (the difference spectrum) corresponds to curve C in the illustration, whose peak is half as high as the first curve, A, and turns out to be situated at about 580 nanometers. After another pause for cone regeneration we repeat the bleaching, this time with a bluish green light of a strength sufficient to give the difference spectrum B, also half the height of A. The maximum of curve B occurs somewhat below 550 nanometers.

These results in the normal eye are what would be expected if there are two cone pigments, one absorbing more in the red (and thus being more sensitive to red light) and one absorbing more in the green. The red bleaching light will remove mainly the red-absorbing pigment and hence give a difference spectrum with a maximum toward the red. The bluish green light similarly will give a difference spectrum with a maximum toward the green.

These two curves, C and B, which are expected in normal eyes and are found in them, should not be found in the eyes of dichromats, according to Koenig's theory. If these color-defective subjects have only one foveal pigment bleachable in the red-green range, then any light that bleaches it 50 percent must do the same thing and have the same result. That is precisely what is found. Half-bleaching by either red or bluish green light results in an identical difference spectrum. This must happen if dichromats have only one pigment that is measurable in the red-green range; it could not happen if they had two or more pigments that were measurably distinct. We may thus conclude with some confidence that dichromats have only one dimension of color vision in the red-green range instead of two because they have only one cone pigment instead of the normal two.

The evidence is strong, therefore, that these dichromats possess only one cone pigment that is sensitive in the red-green range, since they consistently produce only one kind of difference spectrum regardless of whether the half-bleaching light is red or green. It is also clear that the pigment in the deuteranope is more red-sensitive than the pigment in the protanope. Hence Koenig's first assumption is justified.

It is much easier to compare various measurements in a single eye than to compare the eye of one person with that of another, because reflection and scattering usually differ between different eyes. Hence to test Koenig's second assumption—that the cone pigments dichromats do possess are normal pigments—we have not simply measured different spectra in various eyes but also used a more reliable approach.

I have mentioned how the rod pigment rhodopsin was proved to be the pigment of twilight vision: when lights of various wavelengths are adjusted in intensity to bleach rhodopsin at the same rate, all appear equally bright by twilight vision. At Florida State University, D. E. Mitchell and I applied the same test to see whether or not the cone pigments chlorolabe or erythrolabe in the dichromat are the pigments of daylight vision in the protanope or the deuteranope. If lights of different wavelengths are adjusted in strength to bleach the pigment at a fixed rate, all should appear equally bright to the dichromat. This experiment can be done with a high degree of accuracy, as I shall now undertake to explain.

It is easy to adjust the strength of a steady light of any wavelength so that it keeps the pigment 50 percent bleached in a steady state. The pigment bleached to this level is continuously regenerating at a fixed rate while it is continuously being bleached by the steady light. Thus when the light intensity is adjusted for equilibrium, bleaching equals regeneration. Now we can change the wavelength of the steady bleaching light and simultaneously change its intensity to the value that is found to keep the pigment still at the 50 percent bleached level. In this way the appropriate energy can be found for each wavelength

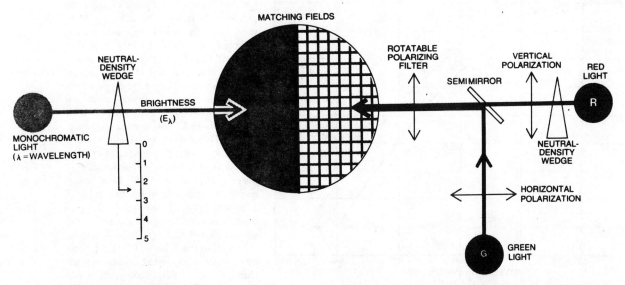

METHOD FOR MAKING RAYLEIGH MATCHES uses an instrument in which a yellow light (*represented by light gray*) is presented in the left half of a field and a mixture of green (G) and red (R) lights is presented in the right half (*green is represented by dark gray*). The G and R beams are polarized at right angles to each other and are mixed to produce a beam that passes through a polarizing filter. By rotating the filter the subject can produce any mixture of green and red needed in order to match the light in the left half of the field. He matches the brightness of the two fields by moving the neutral-density wedge in or out of the left-hand beam.

that bleaches at this constant rate. How about the appearance of brightness?

The dichromat is presented with a field divided into two halves; the left half is filled by yellow light of adjustable intensity; the right half is filled sequentially by bleaching lights of various wavelengths, from 540 nanometers in the green part of the spectrum to 650 nanometers in the red, all adjusted to maintain the pigment steadily at the 50 percent level. The dichromat cannot distinguish in color the yellow from the various bleaching lights; hence he can make a perfect match in each case by simply adjusting the intensity of the yellow. The result he gives is this: those lights that had been found to bleach equally fast (since they each kept the pigment in equilibrium at the 50 percent level) all need the same intensity of yellow for a perfect match. Thus lights that look equally bright to our dichromat bleach equally fast the pigment chlorolabe or erythrolabe that we measure in his eye.

This proves that the chlorolabe in the protanope and the erythrolabe in the deuteranope is the pigment with which that subject sees in the red-green range. The experiment also gives us the spectral sensitivity of these two pigments, since at wavelengths where the sensitivity is doubled the light energy for bleaching can be reduced by half, so that in general the sensitivity is the reciprocal of the energy needed to produce a constant bleaching rate [*see curves 1 and 4 in illustration below*].

The idea that protanopes are "red-blind" has long been widely held, since they find red lights dim. The fact that they lack erythrolabe accords well with this view. Many people have nonetheless found difficulty in accepting the symmetrical idea that deuteranopes lack chlorolabe, since deuteranopes experience no corresponding dimness in the green part of the spectrum. The asymmetry lies, however, in the shapes of the absorbance spectra of the two pigments, as is shown in the illustration on page 70. Nearly all the light at 650 nanometers or longer is absorbed by erythrolabe (peaking at about 575 nanometers). Hence the protanope, who lacks this pigment, will catch little light in the red and will be "red-blind." But the absence of chlorolabe (peaking at about 540 nanometers) still leaves erythrolabe absorbing well in the middle of the spectrum, so that the deuteranope, even though he lacks chlorolabe, is not "green-blind." He can still see this light as being bright, although he cannot distinguish its color from red.

Let me summarize the facts about dichromacy. Instead of having two kinds of cone pigment in the red-green spectral range protanopes and deuteranopes have only one. They accordingly have only one dimension of color in this range.

The spectral sensitivity of a protanope is the same as that of his cone pigment chlorolabe; the spectral sensitivity of a deuteranope is the same as that of his cone pigment erythrolabe. This spectral sensitivity is best measured by matching lights of equal brightness, and it is now well established.

The majority of color defectives are not dichromats, however. They need a mixture of three spectral lights to match all the colors of the spectrum, but they do not mix them in normal proportions. The first important step in classifying these anomalous trichromats was taken by Lord Rayleigh, who asked them to match a spectral yellow with a mixture of red and green. The anomalous subjects fell into two classes: the protanomalous, whose red-plus-green mixture is too red by normal standards, and the deuteranomalous, whose mixture is too green.

Some have considered that the protanomalous need more red in their mixture because, although they have normal cone pigments, the red signals are too weak. Perhaps there is too little erythrolabe in their cones; perhaps the erythrolabe is mixed with chlorolabe; perhaps the generator of red signals is too feeble; perhaps there is some abnormality in the nerve-processing network. We shall argue that none of these things can account for the condition; it must be due to an abnormal cone pigment.

The necessary condition for a red-plus-green mixture to match a given spectral yellow is for each of the cone pigments to receive the same quantum catch from the yellow field as from the red-plus-green field. Clearly if neither pigment can distinguish the two fields, nothing else can, and they will be indistinguishable. Thus a Rayleigh match that satisfies normal subjects must produce an equal quantum catch from both fields in both of the normal cone pigments. Therefore if anomalous trichromats have normal pigments (whether they are separated or partly mixed), these pigments too will have equal quantum catches from the two fields of a normal Rayleigh setting. If the pigments cannot distinguish the fields, the subject cannot distinguish them, and he will say that the fields match. That, however, is precisely what anomalous trichromats deny; they make quite a different setting, which they consistently say is the match for them. Therefore they must have an abnormal pigment, and we should like to know what it is. It has proved quite a tricky problem to iden-

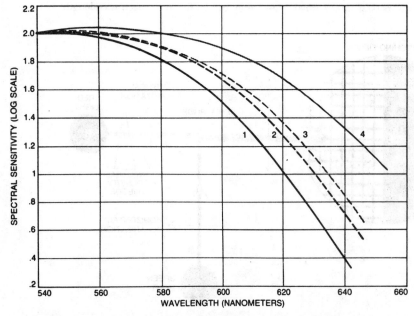

ANOMALOUS PIGMENTS in cones of anomalous trichromats have absorption curves between those of chlorolabe (*1*), the normal green-sensitive pigment, and erythrolabe (*4*), the normal red-sensitive one. Protanomalous trichromats have cones containing anomalous pigment protanolabe (*2*) in addition to cones containing chlorolabe. Deuteranomalous trichromats have cones containing deutanolabe (*3*) in addition to cones containing erythrolabe.

tify this anomalous pigment, but after some 10 years of trials we seem to have got the answer.

Our first hope, naturally, was to be able to harness reflection densitometry to discover anomalous cone pigments in anomalous eyes. This failed entirely to give the answer. The protanomalous gave results indistinguishable from those in the protanope. The protanomalous subjects had the chlorolabe of the protanope but no other detectable pigment. They obviously did have a second pigment, since they could distinguish red from green with certainty, but it was either too scarce to show up or too similar to chlorolabe for separation. The nature of the separation that was tried was to bleach either with deep red light or with bluish green light and to measure the resulting difference spectrum over the range of wavelengths that had proved successful in the normal eye. If the two pigments are quite similar, however, they will be affected almost equally by the two bleaching lights. And the small change in the proportions of similar difference spectra will give rise to only a second-order small change in the difference observed.

Results with deuteranomalous subjects were similar; only an erythrolabe difference spectrum could be seen. One pigment was the same as the pigment in the deuteranope; the other pigment eluded detection, either through its scarcity with respect to erythrolabe or through its similarity to erythrolabe. Since densitometry will not give the answer, we need a different approach. Diane Spitzer Powell, Keith White and I have developed such an approach in our laboratory at Florida State University.

A protanope can exactly match any green presented to him with any red, simply by adjusting the red's intensity. Hence if we neatly exchange the matching red for the given green, he will not know that the substitution has been made. The explanation, of course, is that his one cone pigment, chlorolabe, catches quanta from the two lights equally and experiences no change in the rate of catch when the colors are exchanged. Suppose now that the exchange of these same lights is presented to the protanomalous who possesses chlorolabe plus an anomalous pigment. He can distinguish red from green and sees the change in color. His chlorolabe cones, however, see no change, so that the detection must have been accomplished by the anomalous cones. We have now an effect that depends on the change in quantum catch of the anom-alous cones only. How can we use this effect to find those cones' spectral sensitivity?

As is well known, if a flash is presented superposed on a luminous background, the flash becomes increasingly difficult to see as the background is made brighter. In other words, the threshold for seeing the flash rises in proportion to the background luminance; this effect is known as the Weber-Fechner law. In our experiments we verified that the threshold for our subject to detect the red-green exchange is likewise raised in proportion to the background luminance. We selected two backgrounds, a red one and a green one, and adjusted their luminance so that they both raised the exchange threshold equally. Then, since only anomalous cones are involved in this threshold detection, backgrounds that are equal in threshold-raising power must be equally absorbed by the anomalous cones.

With this procedure one can critically adjust the intensities of any two lights in the red-to-green part of the spectrum (say R_1, with a wavelength of 640 nanometers, and G_1, with a wavelength of 540 nanometers) so that they are equally absorbed by the pigment of the anomalous cones. By establishing the critical intensities for various pairs of wavelengths one can infer the spectral sensitivity of the anomalous pigment. A more reliable method, however, is to make perfect Rayleigh matches for lights of various wavelengths. The threshold rise due to the change in background luminosity depends on nerve organization, but as we have seen color matches depend only on pigments. Thus the method of matches is more secure in interpretation besides being more accurate in execution. Any spectral light of some wavelength, lambda, between R_1 and G_1 can be matched in color by a suitable mixture of R_1 and G_1, the critically adjusted pair.

In making these Rayleigh matches we use an apparatus [see *illustration on page 71*] in which R_1, polarized vertically, and G_1, polarized horizontally, are brought together to form a single beam that is passed through a polarizer. By rotating the polarizer one can vary the ratio of R_1 to G_1 in the common beam. When rotation of the polarizer increases the green component, there is an equivalent decrease in the red component. Since the anomalous pigment catches as many quanta of R_1 as of G_1, the red and green lights exactly compensate, so that the catch is the same in this pigment whatever the R/G proportion.

The R/G mixture appears in the right half of the bipartite field the subject sees in our apparatus. The color in the left half of the field is simply the monochromatic light of wavelength lambda. The subject trims the brightness of lambda by adjusting the position of an extinction wedge so that the two halves appear identical. From calibration of the instrument we know the intensity, E_λ, of the lambda light at the setting that matches the R/G mixture. Then, since the light mixture on the right side is always absorbed by the anomalous pigment to a fixed extent, the monochromatic light E_λ on the left is also absorbed by this pigment to that same fixed extent and E_λ is the intensity required. Thus we know at each wavelength the light intensity resulting in a fixed quantum catch in the anomalous pigment, and this gives us at once that pigment's spectral-sensitivity curve.

The method for protanomalous subjects can be applied in the same way to deuteranomalous subjects and to normal ones. The exchange between red and green lights that look identical to deuteranopes is the exchange that cannot be detected by erythrolabe cones. It is therefore detected only by the green-sensitive cones of deuteranomalous or normal subjects. The intensity of a red background that raises the thresholds for these green cones as much as a fixed green background does is the red intensity that is absorbed by these green cones as much as the fixed green background is. We then make Rayleigh matches equating various monochromatic wavelengths in turn to a red-green mixture, with the primaries G and R set for equal absorption. The energy found to make the perfect match at each wavelength is the reciprocal of the spectral sensitivity of the green-sensitive pigment at that wavelength.

The green pigment in the normal eye, when it is measured in this way, was found to coincide with the chlorolabe, the only pigment in the protanope (in the red-green range), as determined by the fixed bleaching-rate technique. In the same way the red-sensitive normal pigment was found to coincide with erythrolabe in the deuteranope. This justifies Koenig's second assumption; hence we can accept with some confidence his brilliant conjecture that the normal green-sensitive and red-sensitive cone pigments are respectively the chlorolabe of the protanope and the erythrolabe of the deuteranope.

In this account it was assumed for purposes of clarity that each kind of cone contains a single visual pigment. It was pointed out that if the normal pigments were mixed in the cones, one could not account for the abnormal vision of anomalous trichromats. If the eye intends to distinguish colors, it would certainly seem a bad start for it to mix together in one cone the discriminating pigments. The eye, however, often looks deeper than physiologists do and exhibits unexpected tricks of organization. The fact remains that, as Edward F. MacNichol, Jr., and his colleagues at Johns Hopkins University have shown, the pigments are not mixed; each cone contains its own single pigment [see "Three-Pigment Color Vision," by Edward F. MacNichol, Jr.; SCIENTIFIC AMERICAN, December, 1964].

The work of MacNichol and his colleagues was a brilliant technical achievement. A microscopic light beam was passed entirely through the pigment of the outer segment of single cones obtained from human or monkey retinas. The alignment could not be made in visible light or the pigment would have been bleached away before the experiment started. Moreover, the measuring beam had to be so weak that the separation of the signal from the noise was a formidable problem. Ultimately the Johns Hopkins workers obtained three spectral curves, one for each pigment: a blue-sensitive pigment with a peak at about 445 nanometers, a green-sensitive pigment with a peak at about 535 nanometers and a red-sensitive pigment with a peak at about 575 nanometers. The three curves are shown in the top illustration on page 68. The colored dots superposed on the green-sensitive and red-sensitive curves represent, on the same scale, our photosensitivity measurements of chlorolabe and erythrolabe

in the normal human eye. In our experiments the pigments were single, and in the Johns Hopkins experiments the cones were single; the coincidence of results means that single cones contain single pigments.

The illustration on page 72 shows the log spectral-sensitivity curves for both the normal and the anomalous pigments in the red-green range. "Protanolabe" [curve 2] is the anomalous cone pigment that protanomalous subjects possess in addition to the normal pigment chlorolabe. "Deutanolabe" [curve 3] is the anomalous cone pigment that deuteranomalous subjects possess in addition to the normal pigment erythrolabe. Color discrimination depends on the differential quantum catch in the two cone pigments. If these pigments are well separated, as they are in normal people, the differential catch varies considerably with change of wavelength. Hence the color appearance changes greatly, particularly in the yellow-green region. The pigments of the anomalous trichromats, however, have curves much closer together, and as a result the difference in their ordinates changes little with change in wavelength. Thus it is hard for these subjects to discriminate colors even when the fields are juxtaposed; when they have to rely on the memory of these difficult perceptions (as in naming colors), the task is harder still.

It is likely that we have oversimplified the classification of anomalous vision, since some protanomalous subjects do not accept the color matches made by others. Hence the anomalous pigment, protanolabe, may vary somewhat from subject to subject. If it does, we now

have a method for measuring it and for studying how it varies.

Thomas Piantanida and Harry G. Sperling of the University of Texas Graduate School of Biomedical Sciences, working simultaneously and independently from us, have obtained results identical with ours. Their method, which was quite different, involved not color matches but thresholds with backgrounds of different colors and intensities. The fact that we both reached the same conclusions about the nature of the abnormal pigments by different paths strengthens confidence in those conclusions.

The experiments described here seem to establish the following main conclusions. (1) In all the defectives considered there is a loss or an anomaly in a cone pigment. The condition cannot be caused by the abnormal processing of responses from normal pigments. (2) Koenig's two basic hypotheses have been substantiated: protanopes and deuteranopes have lost one cone pigment in the red-green range, and the remaining cone pigment is normal. (3) The pigments chlorolabe and erythrolabe that we can measure by densitometry in dichromats are the pigments with which they see, since lights of different wavelengths that bleach equally fast look equally bright. Therefore these are also the pigments responsible for cone vision in the normal eye. (4) The abnormal cone pigments in anomalous trichromats have at last been measured. In each type of anomalous trichromat the sensitivity curve of the anomalous pigment lies very close to the sensitivity curve of the normal pigment in that eye, thus explaining why color discrimination is difficult for these subjects.

24 👁 -OPENING QUESTIONS

300 physicians and 250 medical students took this quiz—
and many had trouble with it. How well can you do?

"The eyes are windows to the soul," says the proverb, but to the trained ophthalmologist the eyes are often windows to the body, as well.

Many conditions and systemic diseases—including diabetes, high blood pressure, liver disease, kidney disease, sickle-cell anemia, cancer, brain tumor, and multiple sclerosis—may show changes in the eye. But although the study of the eyes (ophthalmology) has reached a high level of sophistication, many common misconceptions about these organs persist, not only among laymen, but among a significant number of trained (but non-eye specialist) physicians, as well. Recently, University of Michigan ophthalmologist Paul R. Lichter gave a quiz to 300 MD's and 250 second-year medical students as part of their postgraduate education program. We've reprinted some of the questions below so you can test your own eye-Q against that of the medical men.

True or False (Answers follow):

1) More people should use an eye wash regularly to clean the eyes.

2) Children should be taught not to hold their books too close when they read, since this can harm the eyes.

3) Astigmatism is a serious eye disorder that often requires special treatments in order to correct.

4) If a patient sees at 20 feet what a normal person sees at 100 feet, then the patient has 20/100 vision.

5) Nearsighted people may outgrow their need for glasses since they will become farsighted as they get older.

6) Children who have difficulty learning to read are likely to have an eye coordination problem; they can be helped with special exercises.

7) Watery eyes are usually of little significance, but may be due to a blocked tear duct.

8) People with weak eyes should rest them often in order to strengthen them.

9) Splashing a small amount of oven cleaner in the eyes could result in severe corneal scarring and permanent loss of useful vision.

10) The need for bifocals indicates an unhealthy state of the eyes.

11) Children with crossed eyes will probably outgrow their condition.

12) Contact lenses can get lost behind the eye, and may even slide into the brain.

13) If children sit too close to the television, they may permanently harm their eyes.

14) People who wear glasses should be checked every year to see if a change is needed.

15) Those who live long enough will need glasses-either for distance vision, near vision, or both.

16) Contact lenses are good for correcting nearsightedness (myopia) so that eventually neither lenses nor glasses will be needed.

17) By moving an object farther from the eye, less accommodation of the lens is needed to see it.

18) Older people who may be having trouble seeing should not use their eyes too much since they can wear them out.

19) Cataracts sometimes grow back after cataract surgery.

20) Wearing glasses that are too strong can cause permanent eye damage.

21) Reading for prolonged periods in dim light can be harmful to the eyes.

22) Headaches are usually due to eye strain.

23) A sign of healthy eyes in old people is their ability to read the newspaper without glasses.

24) Diabetic retinopathy is one of the leading causes of blindness in the United States.

Answers:

1) False. The less that is put into the eyes, the better (except for those who gain economically). 2) False. Holding books close in order to read is common in children. They have a great amount of lens accommodation (the ability to focus on near objects) and can keep close things in sharp focus. Although in rare instances this could also be a sign of severe nearsightedness, in any case, no harm can come of it. 3) False. 4) True. 5) False. All individuals become presbyopic with age. This has nothing to do with nearsightedness or farsightedness. 6) False. 7) True. 8) False. Eyes which are "bad" for whatever reason did not become so from overuse, and can in no way be improved by rest. 9) True. 10) False. 11) False. Crossed eyes in children is always serious and the condition should never be ignored in the hope that the crossing will disappear. Some children have *apparent* but not truly crossed eyes. In such cases the apparent crossing is due to a broad bridge of the nose and as the child grows, this will lessen and disappear. 12) False. The conjunctiva, the membrane that lines the inner surface of the eyelid, prevents a contact lens from passing behind the eye. 13) False. See answer 2. 14) False. 15) True. 16) False. Only *incorrectly* fitted contact lenses will change the shape of the cornea and give the appearance of having corrected nearsightedness. However, this type of treatment should never be allowed since it can cause permanent damage to the eyes. 17) True. 18) False. The eyes are made for seeing and there is no way that they can wear out. 19) False. Since a cataract is an opacity in the lens of the eye, and since the standard cataract operation involves removal of the entire lens, the lens (and therefore the cataract) cannot grow back. 20) False. Since glasses are hung in front of the eyes, looking through them cannot cause harm. However, incorrectly prescribed glasses may result in blurred vision, which causes discomfort and can lead to headaches. 21) False. Although reading in dim light may be difficult and uncomfortable, the eyes are not hurt by it. 22) False. Headaches may be related to eye strain in some cases, but to say they are usually caused by eye problems is an exaggeration. 23) False. Nearsighted individuals can always read without glasses no matter what their ages. Sometimes, a cataract will cause an eye to become nearsighted, resulting in what is called "second sight." 24) True.

FOCUS...

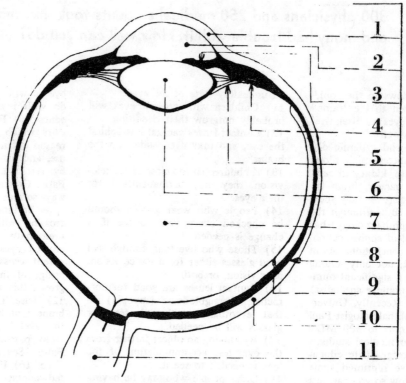

Figure 1. Simplified cross section of the human eye: 1. Cornea; 2. Anterior chamber; 3. Iris; 4. Ciliary muscle; 5. Zonule fibers; 6. Lens; 7. Vitreous; 8. Choroid; 9. Retina; 10. Sclera; 11. Optic nerve.

THE HUMAN EYE

THE HUMAN EYE is built very much like a camera; actually, a TV camera. It is hooked up to the brain by a sort of co-axial cable, the optic nerve. The image received by the eye is relayed to the brain by an electronic impulse sent down the *optic nerve.* Several relay cables in the brain then transfer the image through the brain to the *occipital lobes* at the back in which the picture is formed.

Three basic coats comprise the wall of the eye. The outer coat, the *sclera,* is of tough, firm fibrous connective tissue which gives durability and resistance to the wall of the eye. Just inside the sclera is a delicate vascular coat, the *choroid,* composed of many tiny blood vessels. The choroid's function is to nourish the inner, photosensitive coat of the eye, the *retina.* After an image is focused on the retina, which is very much like the film in a camera, it transforms the light impulses coming to it from the outside world into an electrical impulse, transmitting it by the optic nerve

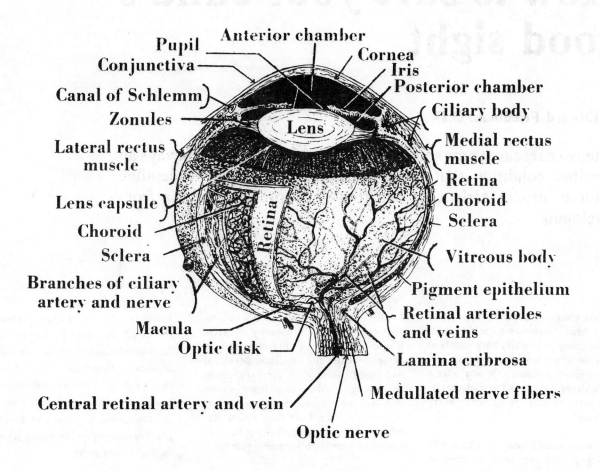

Pupil
Conjunctiva
Canal of Schlemm
Zonules
Lateral rectus muscle
Lens capsule
Choroid
Sclera
Branches of ciliary artery and nerve
Macula
Optic disk
Central retinal artery and vein

Anterior chamber
Cornea
Iris
Posterior chamber
Ciliary body
Medial rectus muscle
Retina
Choroid
Sclera
Vitreous body
Pigment epithelium
Retinal arterioles and veins
Lamina cribrosa
Medullated nerve fibers
Optic nerve

Lens
Retina

Internal structures of the human eye.

to the *optic pathways* of the brain.

The center of the eye is filled with a clear, jellylike substance known as the *vitreous humor*. The front portion of the eye is covered with a perfectly clear watchglass structure, the *cornea*. The cornea serves as the window of the eye.

Just behind the cornea is a compartment, known as the *anterior chamber,* which is filled with a clear fluid, the *aqueous humor*. The *iris,* which gives the eye its color, forms the back portion of the anterior chamber. Basically, the iris serves as the diaphragm of the ocular *camera.*

The hole in the center of the iris is the *pupil*. Under bright light, the pupil becomes small so that less light is admitted. In the dark, the pupil dilates widely, allowing all possible light to reach the inside of the eye. Just behind the pupil is the *lens* of the eye. It is a clear tissue suspended from the rim of the eye by many little "guy wires" known as the *zonules of Zinn*.

How to save your child's good sight

by Edward Friedman, O.D.

Extensive research now shows that nearsightedness is not always an inherited condition that can't be escaped; even in susceptible children, proper early care can frequently prevent myopia from developing.

Have you ever wondered why so many people need eyeglasses these days? Or why so many youngsters have excellent vision for years and then suddenly develop a visual problem? Or why after a child's vision is corrected with glasses he or she keeps needing stronger lenses every few years?

It is a fact that more young people are now wearing glasses than was the case in earlier years. And many doctors, concerned with the increased incidence of nearsightedness, have begun to challenge long-accepted theories as to its cause and the best treatment for it.

A number of eye specialists now strongly support the approach to myopia prevention through vision care which my colleague and I have followed for some time. Over the years the work in preventive care has been increasingly successful, and various programs have recently been formalized which may alter long established guidelines for the use of "corrective" glasses for myopia.

For years, myopia, or nearsightedness, as it is commonly called, was thought to be an inherited condition often first detected in children—which gradually worsened over a period of several years. In virtually all cases, once a child became nearsighted and began to wear corrective lenses, he continued to require them—usually stronger and stronger ones, until the condition leveled off and stabilized in young adulthood.

I believe, and recent work bears out my conviction, that in the majority of cases, a susceptibility to myopia often can be detected before the condition develops, and can frequently be prevented from developing. Further, experience shows that even patients who are already nearsighted can often have their vision stabilized rather than experiencing its continuing deterioration for many years.

Evidence from other researchers now also indicates that myopia need not always be an inherited and inescapable condition. Some investigators now theorize that a person may inherit a susceptibility to myopia but the actual development of the condition and the rate of progression may depend strongly on visual habits, nutrition and environmental factors. Put simply, boys and girls can be taught to limit or avoid nearsightedness.

The key word is prevention. Most of us are acccustomed to consulting a doctor only when a problem presents itself. For this reason, eye doctors rarely see patients with normal vision and they therefore cannot prevent the development of a given condition.

All children should receive their first of a regular series of visual examinations during the preschool years, before myopic problems are likely to develop. Then, comparing the findings on subsequent visits, it is possible to detect a problem right at its beginning.

As a part of every patient's initial evaluation, proper visual hygiene should be discussed. In addition, parents should learn simple tests which they can perform at home to detect changes in their children's vision between checkups. The goal is to identify those youngsters who are susceptible to myopia at the earliest possible time so that preventive action can be begun right away.

You can help your child to develop habits which will help him maintain his good vision. First read the following thirteen points, and then teach your child to follow them:

1. Reading materials should be held no closer to the eyes than fourteen to sixteen inches.

2. Provide adequate lighting for reading, avoid glare. Full lighting for all indoor visual activity is beneficial.

3. Good posture is essential while reading.

4. The reading material should be tilted up so that it is nearly parallel to the face—that is, a book should not lie flat on the desk or table.

5. Books should be held so that the left and right side of the pages are equally distant from the eyes.

6. If possible, avoid reading small print or poor quality print.

7. During long periods of reading, occa-

How To Save Your Child's Good Sight, Edward Friedman, O.D., *Parent's Magazine*, Vol. LII No. 2, February 1977. ©1977 Parent's Magazine Enterprises, Inc.

sionally look up and focus on a distant object for at least five seconds (relaxing your eyes) before resuming close reading. In looking up, the farther away you fix your gaze, the better.

8. Take occasional breaks from prolonged reading, whenever possible, before resuming close work. During these occasional breaks, rotate your eyes in a wide circular pattern for 30 seconds.

9. Avoid the use of small screen television sets, sit at least eight feet from the set, and maintain full room lighting while viewing.

10. Outdoor activities which involve long distance vision, should be encouraged.

11. When spending a long period of time in a restricted visual space such as a small room, occasionally focus at a distance, looking out a window.

12. Avoid squinting, squeezing your lids, or straining to see objects clearly. Try to look at objects in a relaxed way. If necessary, move closer to a blurred object to improve it's clarity. At no time. squint or strain to improve your vision.

13. Whenever possible, avoid reading in a moving vehicle. If reading cannot be avoided, raise your eyes frequently to gaze at the distance.

in a moving vehicle. If reading cannot be avoided, raise your eyes frequently to gaze at the distance.

Developing proper visual hygiene habits at a young age is likely to keep many youngsters from developing visual problems. However, the youngster, adolescent or young adult heavily involved in close work may still be susceptible to myopia and may require more specific visual control activities for practice at home. Several recent studies have shown that a significant percentage of nearsighted people can prevent the condition from progressing by avoiding the traditional use of corrective lenses, and by following instead one of several treatment plans. Promising results have been obtained with various drug therapies (including atropine and phenylephrine), preventive (not "corrective") reading lenses, hard contact lenses, bifocals and the use of a program of visual training. The early warning signs of myopia are listed below:

1. *Accommodative Inertia:* After extended periods of near-point viewing, particularly reading, have the child raise his eyes and focus at a target at least twenty feet away. If he expe-

KINDERGARTEN CHART

2. ETIOLOGY

riences a momentary blur on the distance target before it appears clearly, he may be developing myopia.

2. *Night Vision:* If distant targets appear less clear at night, the youngster may be developing myopia.

3. *Squinting.* If distant objects become clearer with squinting, the child may have myopia.

4. *Viewing Distance:* If a child's vision is clearer when sitting closer to the television than when sitting at the opposite end of the room, he may have myopia.

5. *Vision Test:* Ask the child to read a small distant sign which is barely legible to a family member **known** to have perfect vision. Test **each** eye separately. This test is even more effective at night.

6. *Pin Hole Test:* If the child's vision for a distant target is improved while looking through a small hole

(buttonhole or other tiny hole) held close to the eye, he may have myopia.

There are now several good tests used for predicting myopia. However, these measurements require instruments not available at home. For this reason, it is strongly advised that all youngsters receive an initial office evaluation by the age of five to establish their visual abilities before problems normally develop.

The eye tests given at school are designed to identify children who already have visual problems, and do not evaluate susceptibility to myopia. In fact, many school districts will refrain from requesting an eye-doctor's examination until the child's vision has decreased to at least 20/40. This policy was presumably implemented in a sincere attempt to avoid the premature use of eyeglasses in an era when preventive vision care was

virtually unknown. However, for today's prevention-minded parents, early detection is a must.

We are only beginning to understand the complicated nature of visual function. The evidence to date strongly suggests that the high and increasing incidence of nearsightedness is due to environmental conditions: the great amount of close work as compared to the use of the eye for distance vision, which was more characteristic of earlier times; prescribing "corrective" lenses at the first sign of myopia; and poor visual habits in general.

Those of us specializing in pediatric vision care believe that with the introduction of simple preventive measures at home and in school, we can preserve the normal vision of untold numbers of youngsters—saving them from the prospect of a lifetime of dependence on corrective lenses.

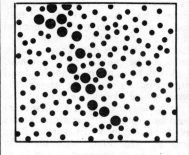

EYE MYTHS

There is a lot that people don't know about eyes. And a lot that they think they know just isn't true. Misconceptions abound. So to set the record straight, Dr. John Eden, a practicing ophthalmologist and author of *The Eye Book,* due this fall from Viking, presents some popular myths about eyes—and the real facts.

MYTH: Wearing glasses will strengthen your eyes.
FACT: Glasses are worn for one of two reasons—to make you see better or to make you more comfortable. But glasses do not correct the intrinsic eye problem. They do nothing to alter the eyes themselves, but simply do their job while worn.

MYTH: Contact lenses prevent an increase in nearsightedness.
FACT: Contact lenses enable you to see normally while you have them on, just as glasses do. But again, that's all they do. They do not, in any permanent way, alter the optics of the eyes. This myth has sprung up because contacts are worn by nearsighted people more than any other group. Nearsightedness usually worsens during the growth period and then levels off around 19 or 20. And contact lenses are often fitted around this time, when nearsightedness tends to stabilize in most people.

MYTH: Measles patients must be kept in a dark room.
FACT: Measles are frequently accompanied by an infection of the cornea which makes the eyes sensitive to light, sore and teary. The patient is more comfortable in the dark, but medically it doesn't make any difference.

MYTH: If you cross your eyes they can get "stuck" that way.
FACT: They don't get stuck, and you can roll them or turn them or twist them any way you like and they'll go back where they belong. There has never been a single case on record where eyes have become stuck.

MYTH: Eating carrots is good for your eyes.
FACT: This myth arose because carrots are a source of vitamin A and it is true that vitamin A is utilized in the physiology of the eye, in light and dark adaptation. Even the most modest American diet, however, contains an abundance of vitamin A— more than the retina can possibly use and then some—and eating additional vitamin A doesn't do any more good. There's a certain amount that is necessary and is utilized and that's it.

MYTH: You should not sit too close to the television or movie screen.
FACT: As far as the health of the eye is concerned, it makes absolutely no difference where you sit, as long as you are comfortable. Of course, if you have to sit close to see correctly, this might be a symptom of near-sightedness and you certainly ought to get your eyes checked. But no damage is caused by sitting close.

MYTH: There's a correct level of light by which to watch television.
FACT: It doesn't matter. If watching television in total darkness is comfortable, by all means do it. It's not healthier or less healthy for your eyes to have dim light in the room, bright light in the right-hand corner, or wherever. Just do what feels right for you.

COLOR BLINDNESS

A common misconception is that color-blind people see everything in black and white. Actually, they can most often see all but a couple of colors, usually red and green. That is why stoplights almost always have the red light on top and green on the bottom—so that color-blind people can tell if it is stop or go simply from the position of the light.

Color-blindness is usually inherited, and it is over 10 times more common among men than women. Studies show that it is also more frequent among people with high blood pressure.

Most color-blind people quickly learn to recognize their problem and adjust to it. But scientists at the U.S. Naval Research Laboratory in Washington have developed a filtered-lens system that allows color-blind people to distinguish colors correctly.

MYTH: Excessive use of the eyes will wear them out.
FACT: You can not harm or injure your eyes in any way by using them as much as you need. If your eyes feel fatigued after a lot of reading, say, just rest them. That doesn't mean there is necessarily anything wrong with your eyes or that you should use them any less.

NIGHT BLINDNESS

People with night blindness are not really "blind" at night. They just adapt poorly to the dark. This condition may be caused by a congenital disease called retinitis pigmentosa.

A far more widespread impairment of night vision has been discovered recently by researchers at the Massachusetts Institute of Technology. They have found that as many as three-fourths of people with normal vision may have night myopia—they become more nearsighted at night. The problem occurs mostly in younger people, says Dr. D. Alfred Owens, a visual scientist at MIT. Only an examination by an ophthalmologist can determine whether a person with normal daytime vision has night myopia. If that is the case, it's easily corrected with the proper glasses to wear at night, especially when driving.

MYTH: Wearing someone else's glasses will harm your eyes.
FACT: It is not going to ruin your eyes. Nothing you put in front of your eyes in the way of lenses is going to cause any optical changes. Don't do it, though—you won't see right and you may get headaches. But you won't cause any alteration in the eyes themselves.

BLIND SPOTS

Everybody has a blind spot in each eye because there are no light-sensitive cells where the optic nerve leaves the inner eye. Usually people are unaware of the blind spot, as the visual field of one eye overlaps the blind spot of the other. People with visual disorders such as glaucoma may also have enlarged blind spots or arch-shaped gaps of vision in the visual field called scotomas.

You can find your blind spot by drawing two half-inch dots a few inches apart on a piece of paper. Cover your left eye and focus on the left dot. Then move the paper sideways away from your face until the dot on the right disappears. It has passed into your blind spot.

Eye Myths, Dr. John Eden, *Harper's Bazaar*, No. 3189, August 1977. ©1977 The Hearst Corporation.

Joy,
Happiness

Man Riding
A Horse

Educational and Vocational Support Systems

Special methods, materials, and equipment must be utilized and combined along with the senses of hearing, touch, smell, taste, and residual vision in order that curriculum might be designed to effectively meet the special educational needs of the visually handicapped person.

The foundation is laid through the acquisition of ability to listen, relate, and remember information to its fullest extent. The educational system takes this into consideration by making the class size small, in order that individual needs may be met on a one-to-one basis. The sense of hearing and touch are sharpened through the use of models of objects so that shape, size, hardness, weight, pliability, surface quality and temperature factors may be acquired. Thus a unified pattern of instruction is formed encompassing stimulation of experience through doing. The student will then be ready to develop further behaviors on his own through self-activity.

Support to this educational foundation is bolstered by the use of braille, and typing. Skills of the command of the environment follow, so that physical and social independence skills may coordinate with orientation factors and mobility acquisition knowledge. The teacher can also employ physical education, reading and writing, listening skills, math skills, social and living skills, use of specialized equipment, adjustable and movable furniture, tape recorders and record players, audio aides, embossed and relief maps, optacon machines, computer translators for braille, embossing systems, compressed speech and the latest prosthetic devices to speed educational progression for the visually handicapped student.

Once educational achievement has been met, how can the visually handicapped person apply his new-found knowledge to acquisition of vocational skills? In much the same manner as the educational process ... technology has carried many of the same machines over into industry, so that the life-process may match educational strides for those with visual problems. Use of lasers, reading machines, copying devices, talking calculators, electronic eyes, and other new devices enable them to become a vital part of the working, producing core of the population at large. These opportunities have been previously denied to the older generation who experienced visual handicaps, but for the fortunate young people who are part of this technological revolution, it will lie with them as to how far these advancements will carry them to further heights of development in the seeing world, and how they carry their new found skills on to those who will follow them.

The gift of vision can never have a price on it — but the promise of advancements of our time and technology must combine with the practical application of the visually handicapped to form a partnership for future generations who might experience similar handicaps.

SOME THOUGHTS ON THE EDUCATION OF BLIND CHILDREN

ROBERT ROTTMAN

Educators today will scarcely question the proposition that modern education is dedicated to the academic and social development of every student to the fullest extent permitted by his individual capacities; that its goal is the graduation of informed, responsible, self-confident, and self-reliant adult citizens who will participate in and contribute to their society. Educational programs for blind children, which serve a particular segment of that total group comprised by "every student," must, of necessity, be imbued with the same philosophy and committed to the same goals.

Society has yet progressed so little in its knowledge of blindness, however, that the question often arises as to what constitutes "the fullest possible extent" for a student who is blind, what measure of information, responsibility, self-confidence, and self-reliance a blind student might reasonably be expected to attain. It is the sincere desire of the National Federation of the Blind to suggest a clear-cut answer to such questions--an answer derived from the experience of thousands of independent, self-sufficient blind adults who constitute the membership of the Federation--and to discuss here a program within the framework of modern education by means of which its worthy ends may be realized, not in part, but in full, for blind students in school today. It is not the intention of the Federation to invade the areas of professional competence of trained educators of blind children, nor to set itself up as an authority on teaching tools and methods. It is rather our earnest wish to be of service to educational programs for blind students by offering the benefit of our collective experience in those areas, beyond the curriculum, of which we are qualified to speak: the nature of blindness, the abilities of the blind, the psychological and sociological implications of blindness in the sighted world of today, and the means to a normal life for blind persons in that world.

Blindness is a physical nuisance and a social handicap. Both of these currently inevitable characteristics begin to affect the life of a blind person from the moment his blindness becomes apparent to himself or to others, even if that moment occurs on the day of his birth. These characteristics of blindness together with their cumulative effect on the developing blind child, are of primary concern to the educator of blind children, for they must constitute the nucleus around which his understanding of the special problems of blind children and his provision for their solution will be formed. Given this understanding and these solutions to supplement a normal school curriculum, a blind child can be expected to achieve, upon graduation, those goals of knowledge, confidence, self-sufficiency, and responsible participation in the work and play of society for which public education today is striving.

The physical nuisance of blindness derives from the fact that most people can see and have organized the physical environment on the basis of the possession and use of vision. Sight is not essential to the performance of the tasks of daily living, but in a world geared to seeing the blind minority must employ "abnormal"--that is, not ordinary--ways of doing many things. Thus a blind infant identifies his mother by footstep, voice, scent, and feel, and his bottle by size, shape, temperature, weight, time of appearance, and--of course--contents. A blind toddler can distinguish the bathroom from the kitchen by size, location, smell, temperature, sound, and--again--contents. A blind child can read and write, in braille, by touch; or with recordings, by hearing.

A blind teen-ager can do geometry, apply make-up, choose clothes, and go out on dates through a variety of non-visual adaptations. A blind housewife can cook, sew, clean house and change diapers; and a blind man can run a lathe, wire a house, manage a business, conduct an experiment, teach a class, or argue and win a legal case.

All of these things can be accomplished without sight; all can be done as well without sight as with it. Sometimes the non-visual methods require equal or even less effort; often they demand extra time, extra concentration, extra exertion, or extra tension. But the important facts are that the methods exist and that they work, that they make of blindness at worst a physical nuisance, but not a physical deterrent.

The implication of these facts for educational programs for blind children is obvious. Such programs, however organized and wherever located, must teach blind children, in addition to the content of the normal school curriculum, the tools and skills which will enable them to fulfill independently, with competence and confidence, the physical demands, not only of school activities, but of normal daily living and competitive employment. This is both necessary and feasible. It is necessary for the simple reason that without such tools and skills, blind students will be extremely limited, if not totally lacking, in the ability to put their education to independent and constructive use. It is feasible because proven tools and skills do exist, and, when competently taught, fit easily and appropriately into the purposeful learning environment of the school; indeed are indispensable--even in school--if this environment includes the expectation of independence, responsibility, and self-direction on the part of students.

The basic physical tools and skills which can make a blind student independent and self-sufficient are not hard to conceive nor difficult to teach. They include such things as the mastery of a system for independent reading, writing, counting, and measuring, which for blind students means braille; the ability to travel independently under all circumstances, which for blind students means the skillful use of a cane plus the employment of other

3. SUPPORT SYSTEMS

senses and common sense; and the general ability to do things for themselves, which for blind students means primarily the long-established habit of planning and organizing. Whether these tools and skills are learned, and, if learned, whether they are used will depend a great deal on the effect of the second significant characteristic of blindness.

Blindness is not only a physical nuisance, which can be readily overcome, but a social handicap which, in our present society, is not so readily removed. The blind as a group are handicapped socially, not because they are essentially inferior, maladjusted, or anti-social, but because people with sight, who constitute a vast majority, grossly over-estimate the physical and mental limitations imposed on the blind by their blindness, and regard the blind as necessarily helpless and dependent, kept alive by the charity of their more fortunate sighted brothers, unable to contribute their share of society's work, and, consequently unentitled to full participation in society's benefits. This feeling is rarely articulated in words, but it speaks for itself in the general actions and attitudes of the sighted toward the blind. The stereotyped concepts of helplessness, loneliness, and utter wretchedness which have been formed about the blind; the pity, wonder, or disgust with which they are regarded; the protective concern which their presence arouses; and the sheltered and limited activities which are organized to occupy their time all bespeak relegation to an inferior status in the eyes of society at large.

The influence of society's attitudes on blind children and blinded adults is strong and pervasive. It extends from infancy to advanced age, and, unless counteracted with a powerful and positive program of education and training, its effect is generally the discouragement of independence and initiative, the limitation of adaptive skills, the development of feelings of inferiority, and, too often, the ultimate acceptance and personification--and thus the perpetuation--of the very stereotype of which the blind are the victims. The over-protection of parents, the pity of friends and relatives, the pessimism of teachers and counselors, and the refusal of employers--all these are at the same time the result and the direct implementation of society's misconceptions about the limitations of blindness; all must be negated, and the strength and desire to resist and surmount them must be instilled in blind students if they are ever to fulfill their potential as self-supporting, fully participating citizens enjoying the same rights and assuming the same responsibilities as their sighted peers.

Tools and skills--while essential--are not enough in themselves to achieve this end, and no educational program for blind children can be considered adequate which confines itself solely to the physical adaptations made necessary by blindness. The major effort of a complete and effective program must rather be directed toward the development in the child--and in the homes, school, and community environment around him--of a full acceptance of blindness without shame and without loss of incentive or aspiration; a firm conviction of the right of the blind to equal status with their sighted peers; an unshakable belief in the ability of the blind to fulfill completely the physical, mental, and social requirements of equal status; a thorough understanding of existing concepts and attitudes about the blind and the barriers to equal status which they present; an unwavering confidence that these barriers to equality can be levelled; and a positive, aggressive determination that these students are going to do the levelling. It cannot be emphasized too strongly that blind students must be equipped with the *confidence* as well as the *competence* to achieve independence and self-sufficiency in a sighted world as yet only too ready to support and "protect" them--at the cost of segregation, dependency, and social and economic inferiority.

All this, then, is to say that the major problems of blindness, at any age, stem from the mistaken attitudes held by the sighted toward that blindness, and from the economic and social impact of those attitudes on the blind. A sound program of education for blind children must first of all free itself from attitudes which limit and discourage; second, help blind students to develop the knowledge, the skills, and the inner strength to meet and overcome these attitudes when they encounter them--as inevitably they must--outside of school; and third, vigorously support and actively assist independent blind persons everywhere, and those who know their true abilities, in a great campaign to educate--and even, where necessary, to legislate--degrading and restrictive public attitudes out of existence.

What does this ringing statement imply for you as an educator of blind children in terms of the program you have organized or are now organizing? What must you do, in addition to meeting the blind child's curricular needs with appropriate special teaching tools and techniques, to instill the confidence and develop the competence so necessary to the survival of his social and economic equality and integrity in an unbelieving sighted world?

The answer lies primarily in the realm of attitudes, specifically in the formulation of a thoughtful, consistent, and vigorous campaign of education designed to accomplish three main objectives: (1) to enable the student to accept his blindness and himself as a blind person; (2) to establish firmly in his mind the conviction that he not only *can* but *should* lead a normal, happy, productive life in full and equal competition with his sighted peers; and (3) to help him to accept and master the tools, skills, and aids that will contribute to his ultimate equality, independence, and self-sufficiency.

With a few possible exceptions, no blind student likes or wants to be blind. Many resist the idea with great determination. Even those who freely call themselves blind may be fighting an inner battle against blindness, a battle that can take the form of hope for a miraculous operation; rejection of anything associated with the special needs of the blind; resentment against parents, school, or the entire sighted population; or the refusal to do anything for oneself. It goes without saying that preparation for life as a successful blind adult cannot begin until the student has come to accept himself as a blind person without loss of self-esteem, and to adopt, confidently and unashamed, the special modes of operating that blindness makes necessary. If the parents have handled their child's blindness well, the chances are that the school will need only to reinforce an accepting attitude

3. SUPPORT SYSTEMS

already established. Unfortunately such instances will be rare, and on the school--as the second great influence in the life of the child--must devolve in most cases the imperative obligation of counteracting--and sometimes flatly contradicting--the home and other influences which have occasioned resistance to blindness in one or more of its forms.

Acceptance of blindness is not brought about in the school environment by repeated lectures on the acceptance of blindness. Instead, the nature of the school environment itself, and the child's relationship with his teachers, will serve as the primary media for an effective conversion. Resistance to blindness is subtly attacked from two closely related points of view, which might be expressed in simplified form as "blind people are normal" and "blindness is not a limitation." The first requires a sincere conviction on the part of the school as a whole, but of the child's teachers in particular, that blind people *are* normal. The very fact that special education programs are provided for blind children can indicate to a particular blind child that he is not unique, that society expects a certain percentage of its children to be blind and considers these children equally worth educating. If the word blind is used freely by the school staff, and the child's blindness treated with quite evident matter-of-factness, and with no lessening of requirements for him because of it; if his special tools and materials and the instruction in the special skills he needs to function adequately are provided as a matter of course; if his outside activities and interests are discussed without wonder, surprise, and undue admiration as they would be with sighted students; if even in the primary grades his future is spoken of with the expectation of a normal life made obvious in such phrases as "when you're in college. . . ," "after you've been on the job awhile. . . ," "your wife may have something to say about that. . . ," "that will come in handy when you're doing your own cooking," or "wait until you're a parent yourself," then the student cannot help but consider himself a normal person. When it is apparent that the school staff, whose opinion in these matters he respects perhaps even more than that of his parents, is not particularly disturbed by his or anyone else's blindness nor holds toward him an attitude different from that bestowed upon his sighted age-mates, then one main objection to blindness is gone.

The second point of attack is closely allied to the first, and is even more important to the bringing about of a true acceptance of blindness. The unshakable conviction that blindness need not limit anyone from anything which makes life worthwhile is the key that unlocks the door of achievement for blind children and for blind adults. It is the foundation upon which every program for the blind which truly meets the needs of the blind has to be built. Blind students, from the very beginning, must be surrounded with this idea, with demonstrations of tools and methods used by blind persons in accomplishing seemingly difficult or impossible tasks; with accounts of the successes of blind persons in such occupations as those of electrician, chemist, physicist, classroom teacher, lawyer, businessman, salesman, farmer, machinist, and homemaker; with the simple, often-repeated statement itself: "Blindness need not bar anyone from anything important in life. Whatever has to be done, there's a way for a totally blind person to do it." (The idea of a totally blind person is important. The students who have the hardest time accepting blindness and the efficient methods of the blind are those with a slight degree of sight, insufficient for the visual performance of most tasks.)

The most effective avenue to the acceptance of blindness, however, is through actual contact with it. The school program should plan and provide numerous opportunities for blind students at every level to meet and talk with self-sufficient, self-confident blind adults from many occupational areas. In no other way can the absence of permanent barriers to normal life be brought home so effectively; in no more convincing manner can blind students learn the value of the skills they are acquiring in a school; from no more competent authority can they get answers to questions about blindness lying long unspoken in their minds; --and from no better source can they learn of the obstacles to integration imposed by society's misconceptions about blindness and the blind.

For these obstacles, too, are involved in the acceptance of blindness. The world of today, a little more sophisticated than it was twenty-five or a hundred and twenty-five years ago, would still rather build a recreation center to fill idle hours than an orientation center to restore self-esteem, self-confidence, and self-sufficiency; would still rather send a newly-blinded wage-earner or professional to a sheltered shop or a vending stand than return him to his former occupation; would still rather drop a daily quarter in a street corner musician's tin cup than trust a competent blind worker with a machine or a decision. The world of tomorrow, barring a miracle or a miraculously effective campaign of public education, will not be drastically changed ten, twenty, even fifty years hence, in spite of the considerable progress that has been made so far by the blind as individuals and as a group. It is important that blind students, as they acquire a firm belief in their own capability, be also arming themselves for the fight to maintain this conviction and to convince the world around them in the face of disbelief, disappointments, and the constant temptation to surrender their dignity and independence in exchange for the meager security of permanent state aid or the limited offerings of a sheltered shop. Made aware from the first of the difficulties imposed by public attitudes, and thoroughly convinced of the injustice thereby done, blind graduates can be helped to develop, not bitterness or resentment, but a realistic evaluation of the hurdles ahead, a compelling sense of the need to surmount them and an aggressive determination not to fall victim to them.

One further consideration for educators in guiding blind students toward their attainment of self-sufficiency remains to be discussed. This is the responsibility of providing for a thorough acquaintance with every available means to the desired end. The importance of a mastery of the physical skills of competence is self-evident. It is taken for granted that no self-respecting educational program would allow a normal blind student to leave without a high degree of proficiency in the reading and writing of standard English braille, considerable skill in the use of a standard typewriter, practice in the use of sighted readers and various types of recorded materials, and, above all, the ability to organize, keep track of, and otherwise assume responsibility for his own material possessions.

3. SUPPORT SYSTEMS

Likewise it is assumed that every program will provide for its students training in the skills of independent travel. Sometimes ignored, but of vital necessity in this regard, is the skillful employment of the long white cane, which gives protection and confidence in moving outside the familiar environment of home and school. Independent travel should be associated with the use of a cane in the minds of blind youngsters long before they begin actual instruction in cane travel techniques in the intermediate grades. Here again discussions with a competent blind adult, who carries his cane with pride and employs it with confident skill, can be of invaluable assistance to both student and teacher in gaining acceptance and appreciation of this indispensable tool of independence.

But the physical skills are not the only aids available to blind students in their efforts to achieve personal independence, competitive employment, normal family life, and the satisfying and constructive use of leisure hours. Society, while failing to recognize its own culpability, has long recognized the state of social and economic inequality in which the blind have traditionally lived. Many programs have been instituted by the states and the federal government, and by private organizations, to ameliorate this unequal condition in one way or another. These programs run the gamut from recreation centers to rehabilitation services, from monetary assistance to missionary efforts; from home teaching to sheltered "homes." Educational programs in which blind students are enrolled must assume the responsibility not only of informing them about every service, every aid to which they are legally entitled, but of helping them to develop, as a part of their overall philosophy of self-sufficiency, that fine discrimination which distinguishes between those offerings based on mistaken charity and the desire to relieve lonely, useless hours with time-filling palliatives, and those services which operate to equalize the opportunities for blind persons to take their places as self-reliant, self-respecting, contributing members of society.

Seeing better with blindfolds

KAY E. AYLOR

TRY THIS: Blindfold yourself. Move through the room and into another room. Ask someone to drop an object on the floor. Now locate the object and pick it up. (A word of caution: Move slowly. Don't jam your fingers groping around, and be careful not to bump your head against a table or chair when trying to pick up the object.)

Had you been enrolled last June in a certain program for teachers of the visually handicapped at the University of Northern Colorado (UNC) at Greeley, you would move with confidence, even agility, through this exercise. The program—known as dual competency teachers for the blind—qualifies its participants to instruct the blind in academic subjects and to train them in the skills they need to move from place to place.

One of the first experiences given to students in the dual training program is "behind the blindfold." According to

Seeing Better With Blindfolds, Kay E. Aylor, *American Education*, Vol. 8 No. 4, May 1972. ©1972 The United States Department of Health, Education and Welfare.

behind a blindfold for 50 hours

Robert Crouse, project director, the blindfolding helps the future teachers better "to understand the mobility problems of the blind person."

The philosophy that supports the dual mobility program, a special project funded by the U.S. Office of Education under Part D of the Education for the Handicapped Act, is aptly stated by Grace Napier, coordinator for all UNC programs that train teachers of the visually handicapped: "What good is 12 years of education to a blind person if at the end of it he can't even get himself to a job?"

As early as 1960 some universities graduated students who were trained to instruct the blind in finding their way about, but these students were not qualified to teach academic subjects. School districts found themselves faced with the costly absurdity of having to hire two teachers—one for academic subjects and one for mobility—in order to train properly their visually handicapped children.

Dr. Napier, who is blind herself, recognized the illogic of the situation and worked hard to help bring about the dual mobility program designed to correct it. The program has a twofold purpose: First, to train graduate students for certification as academic teachers and also mobility teachers for blind children; second, to increase the number of qualified "mobility" teachers in the Rocky Mountain area. Although the UNC program cannot require graduates to remain in the Rocky Mountain region, its recruiting makes the point that such a decision would be desirable. And there is a reason for this concern.

The region's rugged topography isolates communities, and school districts consequently are small and usually operate from a limited tax base which severely restricts support for special education. There are 225 known visually handicapped children in day school programs in Colorado, but in any one school district there might be only enough children to support one or two teachers. Few districts can afford both an academic teacher for the blind and a mobility teacher for so small a number of children. Even training regular classroom teachers to work with visually handicapped children imposes a difficult if not impossible financial burden upon the districts.

Because of this restricting condition many visually handicapped youngsters in Colorado have only one recourse: to enroll in the residential State School for the Deaf and Blind at Colorado Springs. Eighty-five children now live there. By training teachers who are academically qualified and also able to teach mobility to the blind, the UNC dual mobility program brings a service to those with visual problems at a cost within the financial capability of most school districts—even if, as in many cases, several districts need to pool their resources. For blind children now of necessity living away from home, dual mobility thus holds forth the prospect of remaining with their families and still receiving the help needed to prepare them to be self-sufficient adults.

The UNC program, new in the field and the only one of its type in the United States, condenses into 15 months a variety of experiences for its enrollees. For instance, the blindfold experience, which is sometimes criticized as being unrealistic, since it cannot teach a sighted person what it's like to be blind. Crouse defends blindfolding as "teaching an awareness of skills the blind need in order to move around." The blind "see"

in a number of ways, he points out. They gather a great deal of information about the environment through other senses. They are acutely aware of sounds and feel temperature changes and air currents that a sighted person wouldn't notice. They sense texture differences under their feet and memorize routes. They form a mental map of where they are. A teacher for the blind needs to know all these basic things to understand how an unsighted person operates and what difficulties he can expect to encounter in certain situations. The blindfold training provides this to the UNC students.

Here's how the blindfold experience works and what the student is supposed to learn from it.

Each student puts on a blindfold for one hour a day for the first ten to 15 weeks he is with the program. At the start Crouse acts as a guide, but as soon as the student learns to use a cane—and this looks a lot easier than it really is—he is on his own. A cane affords some measure of assistance, but dependence upon it can be an unnerving experience, especially when the process of finding one's way around is complicated by such rather innocuous seeming things as autumn leaves (they cover curbs and cause slippery places), snowbanks and rough or uneven terrain (they tend to divert the sightless person from his course), and dogs and cats dashing across the path (they are startling and many times cause the blind to lose their orientation).

During his many hours behind the blindfold the student is placed in a variety of situations and environments, including riding an escalator, purchasing an item in a department store, and navigating the campus. Crouse believes in letting a student make mistakes as he moves through the different situations. The reason: Once the student is out teaching, his students will in turn tend to make those same mistakes, and the teacher will be better equipped to correct them and to guide his students into a pattern for effective locomotion.

Says Jan Floyd, one of the students in the present class, "Most of us were baffled by the blindfold experience until we got a handicapped child of our own to instruct. Then, because we had some small notion of what it was like not to be able to see, we could guide our students in a more intelligent and understanding way."

There are other aspects to the dual mobility training. For instance, each of the program's enrollees works with at least one "client"—meaning a visually handicapped person—teaching him the skills of mobility under the direct supervision of Crouse. Most of the clients are students enrolled for academic study at UNC. An arrangement with the physical education department provides for the clients to receive two credits in physical education for participating in the project. Aside from helping the teacher trainees, this aspect of the program benefits the clients too, familiarizing them with the campus and the town. For some, it is their first opportunity to learn mobility under professional guidance.

The four students presently enrolled in the program, having completed their blindfold training, were given an opportunity for equally useful instruction. With Crouse they traveled east to survey other efforts serving the blind. At Seeing Eye, Inc., in Morristown, New Jersey, they saw the operation of an organization that uses guide dogs for the blind. They also had a chance to observe the services of a large voluntary agency, the Lighthouse in New York City. They visited the facilities for the blind at the Perkins School in Watertown, Massachusetts, and at Massachusetts Institute of Technology they learned firsthand about current research relating to the causes of visual handicaps and the problems accompanying them. The climax of the trip came at the Walter Fernald School, a State institution for the retarded in Massachusetts, where the students visited a pilot study on teaching mobility to severely retarded blind people.

Requirements for the UNC dual mobility training project are not extensive, consisting of regular credentials for admission to graduate school at the university plus near normal vision, a standard set by The American Association of Workers for the Blind, which certifies all mobility teachers.

Enrollees in Northern Colorado's dual mobility program receive an assistantship provided by the USOE grant under which the program operates. The $49,118 grant for the current school year covers student compensation, staff salaries, and teaching needs for the project.

Since as many as 30 applications may be received for the project, as against only four or five positions for new students, the job of screening candidates can be intense. Although teaching experience is not a requirement, those who have it, either in a regular classroom or in a special education situation, are favored.

Not every person is capable of enduring the rigors of five quarters of intensive preparation for academic/mobility teaching of the blind. The course is demanding and time consuming, and generally leads to a job with similar characteristics—that of an itinerant teacher who must travel long distances in thinly populated territory to serve a limited number of children, with a salary for one job and an output for two. Such disadvantages are evidently more than offset by the intangible inner rewards that derive from serving those who need special help, for applications for the dual mobility program keep coming.

Members of the program staff foresee that other programs might adapt some of the techniques used in the UNC program—the blindfold experience, for example, and the practical work with "clients" throughout the training period. Meanwhile they are concentrating on increasing the number of teachers in the Rocky Mountain region who can teach the blind in both academic subjects and mobility—toward making sure that the youngster who can't see very well and hasn't been able to learn much will now receive the kind of training that will prepare him for a job in his community and show him how to get to it.

Liberating The Blind Student

Steve Hulsey

Ed Bordley is a junior at Casear Rodney High School near Dover, Delaware. He is totally blind. He is also a champion wrestler, an honor student, a member of the student council, and a discus thrower and shot putter on the track and field team.

Ed Bordley illustrates a proposition that officials of Delaware's Department of Health and Social Services believe teachers and school administrators everywhere should understand: That blind youngsters can handle regular classrooms in regular schools with considerable benefits to themselves and no special problems for their teachers or their classmates.

At first, of course, both they and their teachers will need some expert preparation. And along the way both they and their teachers also may occasionally need some expert help. In Delaware such backup is provided by what is called the Itinerant Teachers program, operating out of the department's Bureau for the Visually Impaired.

Traveling from district to district in the little Diamond State—Delaware contains only three counties—the itinerant teachers serve 55 students in grades three through 12 variously enrolled in public, private, and parochial schools. Five of the 55 are totally blind and the remainder "legally" blind—that is, they have ten percent or less of normal vision, or peripheral vision of 20 percent or less. Such children see at 20 feet what normally sighted persons see at 200 feet, and they are unable to read books printed in normal-sized type.

Ed Bordley, who was blinded by a detached retina at the age of nine, is now one of the 55. Previously he had been attending a residential school for the blind—in another State, since Delaware maintains no such institutions. For the past two years, thanks to the Itinerant Teachers program, he has been living at home with his parents, attending public school, and as his record demonstrates, holding his own with his sighted classmates.

Norman Balot, deputy chief of the Bureau for the Visually Impaired and supervisor of the Itinerant Teachers program, does not denigrate the quality of education offered in residential schools, and blind students are referred to them as the situation warrants. Their drawback, he says, is that they remove the child from the normal psychological and social development which the sighted youngster living at home and going to the local public school takes for granted. Balot himself attended a residential

She uses Braille, but otherwise Laura Brower seems to be just another student at Delaware's Linden Hill Elementary School

school—he has been totally blind since the age of three—and one of his chief recollections is the isolation of residential students from youngsters attending "regular" schools nearby. Much has changed in residential schools during the intervening 25 years, he says, but in any case he believes that the option should rest with the children and their parents—that these youngsters should be free to choose.

"The blind child has a *right* to attend the public school in his district if he so desires," Balot says, "just as other children do."

The move toward providing that option in Delaware began in 1957 when the State's Department of Public Instruction and the Wilmington School Board established a Resource Teaching program to provide special equipment and individual attention to visually impaired students. The arrangement calls for such youngsters to be bused from their "home" districts to a public school in Wilmington, where they have their own classroom and their own special teacher. Balot feels that while this program represents an important step forward, it doesn't go far enough in opening up the options. Blind children who want to do so, he says, should be given full opportunity to interact freely with their classmates.

As an extension of the Resource Teaching program he proposed the Itinerant Teacher program with the goal of providing a mechanism for integrating as many blind children as possible into the regular public school system. Teachers enlisted into the program would have the twin assignments of winning acceptance on the part of teachers and administrators and then providing support both to the students and to their teachers in overcoming any difficulties that might arise.

The program was launched in 1970 with one itinerant teacher

Discus-thrower Ed Bordley's blindness does not prevent him from being a fine athlete and (bottom photo) an outstanding student in classrooms with sighted students.

and Secondary Education Act and Part B of the Education of the Handicapped Act. The hope is that the State will provide support entirely on its own in the near future, and the success of the program has in fact enabled it to move significantly in that direction. In 1970 Delaware was sending 20 children to out-of-State residential schools for the blind at a cost of $7,100 each. Today, with the Itinerant Teacher program, only nine Delaware children are attending such schools, and State officials estimate that between 50 and 60 students can be educated in public schools at an approximate overall cost of $40,000 — a significant saving.

Many factors are responsible for that success, Balot says, and prominently among them are the itinerant teachers themselves — Stephen Zacharkiw, Michael Czerwinski, and Mary Ann Bennett. All are certified public school teachers with special training or experience in working with the blind. The format calls for each itinerant teacher to work with 20 students.

Though the itinerant teachers are the focal point of the instructional aspects of the program, numerous other people make important contributions. Some 30 volunteers devote large amounts of time to typing large-print and Braille textbooks, the students' most important learning tools. The bureau staff includes an educational counselor who works closely with the children and their parents in helping them adjust to blindness and chart their future course. And increasingly the program is capturing the enthusiasm and support of school counselors and teachers — an example being Peggy Fiske at Caesar Rodney High, who is learning Braille so she can work more effectively with Ed Bordley in his Spanish lessons.

Teacher and school administrator attitudes nevertheless remain a basic issue, the problem being one not of antagonism to the program but concern for the students, perhaps even over-concern.

"The hardest thing for them to accept," says Zacharkiw voicing a common observation among the itinerant teachers, "is that a blind youngster can and should be treated like every other student and not as someone special." School officials are quite naturally fearful that a blind child might be injured, and they assume that such children will be unable to keep up in classes that involve the use of various kinds of equipment — typing classes, for instance, or shop or home economics. Zacharkiw insists, however, that no school subject has yet been encountered that a blind child can't handle — perhaps not in the same manner as a sighted child but in a manner that is nonetheless educationally valuable.

Gym classes have presented a particular problem, the assumption by most gym teachers being that a blind child is

and 20 youngsters. Two teachers and 45 children participated during the second year, and currently three teachers are working with 55 students in 22 of Delaware's 26 public school districts plus a few private and parochial schools. The experience, Balot says, is a two-way street. Blind students get an invaluable start in developing self-reliance and self-sufficiency, and their sighted classmates get a new understanding of blind people and a new appreciation of their capabilities.

To date the program has been supported by a combination of State funds and Federal grants under Title I of the Elementary clearly out of his element. Zacharkiw argues that while blind youngsters admittedly have trouble shooting a basketball through the hoop, they can learn to dribble excellently. If healthful physical exercise is the objective, he says, they have a place on the court, and through demonstration workouts with blind children in the gym, he has managed to persuade several resistant teachers to change their minds. One girl has even been admitted to an archery class. Her gym teacher placed a transistor radio on top of the archery target, and the girl scored very well by shooting toward the sound, the only problem being that she sometimes hit the radio itself.

Zacharkiw emphasizes that the resistance he and the other itinerant teachers encounter does not seem to be based on rejection but on a combination of compassion and unawareness. Not understanding the capabilities and motivation of blind youngsters, he says, the teachers tend to become so over-protective that they underrate the ability of these youngsters to fend for themselves and overlook the need to encourage them to do so.

James Schoch, principal of Caesar Rodney High concludes that he had some of these feelings when he was first approached about enrolling Ed Bordley. Schoch was at that time new to his position and was faced with a school-wide discipline problem. He was reluctant to take on another burden.

He was concerned, he says, about how the boy would find his way about in the school's large physical plant and the problems teachers would have in trying to teach a single blind student in a normal classroom setting. "But I guess my chief worry," Schoch says, "was for the boy's safety, particularly at those times, for instance, when the 1,700 students were changing classes."

After considerable soul-searching, weighing the potential benefits against his apprehensions, Schoch agreed to give the arrangement a try. Bordley has subsequently not only become a valuable member of the student body but has given Schoch and other members of the staff an impressive demonstration of how self-reliant blind students can be.

"I was talking with him in my office one day," the principal recalls, "and after we had finished I offered to walk him back to his class but he declined. At that time I was still concerned about him, though, so I followed him. He casually walked down the hall, taking about five different turns, and up the stairs and into his classroom with no difficulty at all."

"I can tell where I'm going by the sounds and by people's voices," Ed explains.

The teachers have similarly overcome whatever apprehensions they had felt and make no special arrangements for teaching him. Any help he needs is provided by the itinerant teachers. His classmates have similarly overcome their reservations. They do not exactly take him for granted, but they do not subject him to elaborate ceremony, either, and they are more likely to identify him as an athlete or a member of the student council than as "the blind fellow."

"Ed is clearly a positive influence here," says Schoch, "both with the teachers and the other students. He is showing us what a person with a disability can do and that we should not set such people aside."

Jennifer Smith, a "legally blind" seventh grader, is making a similar impression at Wilmington's Talley Junior High School. Her mother says that Jennifer is holding her own academically and is probably doing at least as well as she would in a residential school. More important, Mrs. Smith says, is the psychological benefit of being able to live at home and remain close with her older sisters.

Jennifer began to lose her sight three years ago. She and her parents opted for the Itinerant Teacher program, and today she is working with Michael Czerwinski, who has helped her learn Braille and how to handle a typewriter, who is always available for tutoring in other subjects, and who in general encourages her to maintain a vigorous, affirmative attitude.

Another case in point is that of Laura Ann Brower, whose father accepted a job transfer to Delaware from Texas only after he learned of the program and that his daughter could participate. Blind since infancy, Laura Ann is now in the third grade and in the advanced portion of her class.

As her parents see it, the program was not simply valuable but essential. "A child that age," says Mrs. Brower, "needs to be with her family."

When children like Laura Ann and Jennifer are referred to the Bureau for the Visually Impaired, usually by the State Department of Public Instruction, the first item on the agenda is a visit by the bureau's educational counselor. The education counselor meets with the student and his or her parents to discuss the child's background and seek to determine what kind of school setting seems most appealing and practical and what special considerations should be taken into account. Following this visit the case is analyzed by a review committee that typically includes, in addition to the educational counselor, one of the itinerant teachers, a school official, a psychologist, and a pupil placement officer from the child's school district; and if the youngster had been attending school before becoming blind, a teacher from that school. The goal of their study is to develop a range of options.

"Generally speaking," says Balot, "we want the children and their parents to understand completely the possibilities and opportunities of three alternatives to have the child attend a special school, to enroll in the Resource Teaching program, or to attend regular school under the Itinerant Teacher program. We make recommendations, of course, but if a particular child and his parents chooses a residential school, we go along with that decision. We don't try to ram our recommendations down anyone's throat."

Those who choose to attend regular school are assigned to an itinerant teacher who immediately begins instruction in Braille, works out a tutoring schedule if tutoring seems called for, and provides the student with basic materials developed for blind students raised graph paper, for example, large-print books, magnifiers. In preparation for formal enrollment, the teacher helps the student become familiar with the school's physical layout tracing with the youngster the routes he or she will take to meet every circumstance during the day. School officials must be satisfied that the youngster is ready to find the way around without special help.

While the itinerant teachers regularly check in with the

students and their teachers, and are available almost immediately in the event of a problem, they try to limit their visits and over the course of time diminish them. The objective is to build self-reliance on the part of the students, and on the part of their classroom teachers as well.

"Particularly at first," says Zacharkiw, "I have to remind the teachers to let the blind children do things on their own, not to give them undue help or consideration.

"For one thing, these children can in effect be taught to be dependent, and that just adds to the problem. And there's another reason. Any student is likely to 'test' the teacher, to see how much he or she can get away with. The blind are no different, but teachers are likely to be more lenient with them. I tell these teachers that the child's blindness is no excuse for not doing the assigned work. Some of the students, of course, do not do very well academically, but their blindness is not necessarily the

reason. They perform below average for the same reasons other students do." By and large, however, the students hold their own. In any case, neither Balot nor the itinerant teachers had supposed that the program would somehow make the blind students more brilliant. Their goal is instead to liberate these youngsters — to encourage them to take charge of their own lives, and to encourage their sighted classmates and their teachers to give them freedom to do so.

FOR MORE INFORMATION

Readers desiring further information should write to: Delaware State Department of Health and Social Services, Bureau for the Visually Impaired, 305 W. Eighth Street, Wilmington, DE 19801.

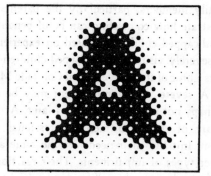

Counseling Families of Severely Visually Handicapped Children

HELEN E. FROYD, M.S.S.S.

*Mrs. Froyd is a clinical social worker
with the Birth Defects Clinic, University
of Colorado Medical Center, Denver.*

ABSTRACT: *Professional counseling can benefit both the severely visually handicapped child and his family. Initially, counseling may be useful to family members as they deal with their immediate reactions to the diagnosis and begin to develop realistic expectations for their handicapped child. When involved, the professional person may continue to provide an essential service. As the severely visually handicapped child faces each developmental task, the route he takes to achievement differs greatly from that used by the sighted child; hence, the uniqueness of the needs of the severely visually handicapped child. This uniqueness, how to deal with it, and what problems arise when it goes unrecognized, are all potential areas in which the professional person may be involved. In addition to these direct services, the professional person may serve as consultant to community agencies willing to work with these children. Unfortunately, persons prepared to meet the needs described are seldom available to the severely visually handicapped child and his family.*

There are two primary reasons why professionals working with visually handicapped children and their families must be concerned with providing counseling for the family on an on-going basis: the child himself and the other family members, particularly the parents. This discussion is an attempt to illustrate how counseling can be of benefit to the parents and to the visually handicapped child; it is based on experiences with young congenitally blind or severely visually handicapped children and their families at the Birth Defects Clinic of the University of Colorado Medical Center.

□ A severe visual impairment may be discovered shortly after birth, but perhaps not until some months later. At whatever point the family becomes aware of the impairment, professional counseling should be available to them. Initially their needs are the same as those of parents of children with other types of impairments. Their reactions may include shock, grief, anger, guilt, and a searching for reasons (Cohen, 1962; Kozier, 1962; Olshansky, 1962). Warnick (1969) discusses the possibility of another reaction, that of hope. She bases this on the belief that expansion of services makes realistic planning possible, thus bringing a degree of hope. Her conclusion is that this feeling of hope may even replace "Chronic Sorrow." Whatever their individual reactions, parents are faced with the difficult tasks of dealing with these reactions, and making adjustments in their daily routine that will affect the total family unit in order to meet the new demands placed on them.

These tasks are frequently complicated by the parents' lack of knowledge and experience with severely visually handicapped people. As a result, they have no conceptual background on which to base their hopes or to control their

Parents' Reactions to Child

Stereotypical thinking

fears. That is, if one's only experience with visually handicapped persons is to have seen a blind beggar or to have heard tales of a "blind genius" (common cultural concepts of blindness), there is no reality-oriented basis on which to build realistic expectations for the blind or severely visually handicapped child.

☐ Additional reality factors serve to complicate the picture and make the task of the parents even more difficult. When the diagnosis of visual impairment or blindness is initially made, it is not uncommon that the amount of vision, if any, that the child has or will have cannot be determined. For example, one child born with familial congenital cataracts had decreasing vision until surgery was possible at one year of age. Initial surgery was followed by additional surgery on two other occasions. When the child was 20 months old, he began wearing glasses. He continues to have extremely limited vision, but the amount of useful vision is quite different than it was at birth. In another child, who had congenital glaucoma, the progression of the disease followed a different course. In spite of ten surgical procedures in the first 18 months of life, he has decreasing vision and faces total blindness.

This period of uncertainty makes it difficult, if not impossible, for the parents to grieve since they are not sure for what they are grieving or to accept since they are not sure what they are accepting. For example, a father whose son had congenital cataracts was quite rejecting of him; he seldom played with him, made unrealistic demands of him, and spoke of him as "hopeless." Following cataract surgery the child made rapid strides in his development and both parents felt his vision had greatly improved. The father's relationship with his son changed markedly at this time; he played appropriately with him, helped with his care, and spoke highly of his accomplishments. However, when the child regressed somewhat during a prolonged period of illness, the father reverted to his former attitude.

Another complicating factor is that a visual handicap may well be accompanied by one or more additional handicapping conditions. Based on a 1968 survey done by the Research Department, American Foundation for the Blind, it was estimated that there are 15,000 multiply handicapped blind children in this country (Graham, 1970). In our clinic, almost half of the visually handicapped children seen in a three-year period had one or more additional handicaps. It becomes apparent that the aspect of medical care for the child, either in direct relationship to the visual handicap or to an accompanying handicap may also be a part of the total picture a family must face at this time. Briefly, then, the birth of a severely visually handicapped child presents the family with what is potentially the most difficult psychological task they may ever have to face; in addition, while struggling with their emotions and feelings, they are also facing new demands on their time and energies. With this in mind, let us consider the blind or severely visually handicapped child.

☐ From the moment of birth each child needs, among other things, acceptance, love, and an environment which enhances and encourages growth. A home in which the adults are struggling with the problems described above does not seem the most likely place to find these things. At precisely the time when the parents may feel the need to withdraw and concentrate on their own needs, they are called upon to give—and not just the usual "tender loving care" that each child needs, but giving that requires initiative and imagination in reaching the child. For example, the response of the young visually handicapped child to the sounds of someone entering the room may be quite different from that of the sighted child. The sighted child turns toward these sounds and soon learns to stretch out his arms in expectation of being picked up. In contrast the visually handicapped child may cease his babbling and kicking

3. SUPPORT SYSTEMS

when someone enters the room and remain perfectly still, only to resume his former activity when left alone again. This is a response which parents frequently interpret as rejection or as an indication that the child is happiest when left alone. Actually the child is attending to or responding to auditory cues. Unfortunately this may discourage the parents from interacting with the child when in fact they need to be more aggressive in establishing a relationship with him.

During the first year of life two additional exciting, yet potentially dangerous, developments occur; these are the beginnings of speech and the discovery of the body. They are exciting because they are so important, but dangerous because for the blind child they can become solely a means of self-stimulation rather than ways of reaching out and communicating. The necessity and importance of the development of speech and language for the blind or severely visually handicapped child is obvious.

A critical period

☐ Words and sounds must, from the very beginning, be presented in a thoughtful and meaningful way. A constant barrage of noise and meaningless words can be damaging, as can long periods of silence. Those nurturing the child must learn to use their voice meaningfully, varying their inflection and volume and the distance from which they speak to the child. Words must be provided as names for objects and descriptions for actions. The beginnings of language occur in the blind or severely visually handicapped child at the same age level as in a sighted child; however, because this child's sources of stimulation are limited, sounds and then words become a source of self-stimulation. If language is to progress beyond this to become a tool for reaching out to the world around him, the child must have objects to touch and identify. It is at this point that a delay may occur because identifying or naming objects, the next step in language development, depends on his being in contact with innumerable objects and being in many places—in short, on being mobile. Mobility, however, comes slowly to the blind or severely visually handicapped child. A comparison of the development of the sighted and blind or severely visually handicapped child serves to illustrate this.

Beginnings of Speech

The sighted child becomes "touch hungry" between three and four months and is stimulated by that which he can reach. The blind or severely visually handicapped child develops the motor pattern for reaching between the fifth and sixth month, but any contact he makes with objects is accidental. However, shortly after this pattern has developed, a random searching for objects begins (Fraiberg, 1968). Reaching is the precursor to creeping. Although the baby may achieve "postural readiness" for creeping (the ability to support himself on hands and knees) between six and eight months, some time may elapse before he actually moves forward. Fraiberg associates this probable delay and subsequent development as being linked to the baby's learning to "reach on sound cue." That is, when the baby associates a sound with an object, reaches for and grasps it, then he is ready to crawl. This is the point at which the child learns to respond to auditory cues in much the same manner as a sighted child of five months responds to visual cues—with the difference that the blind child arrives at this point of development by a more difficult route somewhere between six and 12 months of age. It can easily be seen, then, that there may be a delay in the development of speech until the baby becomes mobile; mobility may be delayed awaiting the development of prehension abilities. Prior to the time when these abilities are integrated (thus making creeping possible), it is essential that the baby be provided with experiences designed to prevent deviation in the development of speech and bodily move-

"Touch hungry"

Auditory cues

ment. These are but a few of the potential areas in which developmental deviations may occur in the very early years of the child's life.

☐ Let us consider now some of the situations I have seen while working in the clinic. Early in my experience I worked with a family composed of a father, mother, maternal grandmother, first son—born with anophthalmia—and now a new baby boy. The problems in this family were many. The mother had been depressed since the birth of her first son and there had been no positive relationship established between the child and any of the adults in the home. The child, Tim, at age 2½ years spent most of his time sitting wherever placed, banging a toy or, more usually, sitting with his right thumb in his mouth and batting his fingers with his left hand. One afternoon Tim, his mother, and I were sitting on the floor introducing Tim to a new toy. Tim had no interest in being disturbed and was vocally making this quite clear. Suddenly his grandmother appeared, quickly picked Tim up, and in German scolded the two of us who were still sitting on the floor. She took Tim with her and held him in her lap while he resumed his thumb-sucking and finger-batting. A rough translation of the grandmother's remark is something like "You must not make him do that; he is happiest alone."

Interference

Somewhat later in my contact with this family, the mother was able to take Tim for a physical therapy evaluation and then bi-weekly sessions in physical therapy. Between sessions there were exercises to be done at home. More memorable than the grandmother's scolding was my first visit in that home after physical therapy sessions had begun. We were sitting on the floor again— the mother, father, Tim, and I. The three of them were demonstrating how they did Tim's exercises, the mother and father joyful about this new development and Tim tolerating the attention fairly well.

A new involvement

☐ In one of the families we have followed there are four children, two of whom are blind. In an effort to help the mother with the children and to broaden their experiences, an aunt volunteered to spend Saturdays with one of the blind children, Mike. She and Mike played in the park, visited department stores, and he began learning to order and pay for their hamburgers at lunchtime. A problem arose, however, when the aunt was unable to come on Saturday. This is a family without a phone, so frequently some days would pass before they knew why the aunt did not appear. The mother tried to explain to Mike that "things come up" and that his aunt would have come if she could. Mike was not able to understand that something could prevent her coming and each time she missed a Saturday it was as difficult for him as the first one. Some conversations with Mike and his mother revealed that he knew nothing about his aunt except that she spent Saturdays with him. For Mike, she had no existence except on Saturday. Magical thinking and confused concepts related to the permanence of objects persist a very long time in children whose environment does not provide auditory information in the absence of visual information. Mike's mother saw the problem as his needing to learn how to handle disappointment. Perhaps, but a large part of learning to handle disappointments was, for Mike, a need for more information—where did his aunt live, did she live with someone, what kind of experiences did she have during the week, and, as soon as available, specific information as to why she hadn't come on Saturday, etc.

Magical Thinking

Just as magical thinking and confusion in regard to the permanence of objects persist, so can the blind child's difficulty in the areas of adaptation and self-assertion. Glen, a very dependent blind 12-year-old boy, has been in school for six years. His school experience has primarily been in a protective one-to-one situation. Recently he has been expected to move from class to class

Adaptation and self-assertion

3. SUPPORT SYSTEMS

and did fairly well until faced with a need to make a decision. Returning from math class he told his teacher he needed to go to the rest room. She gave him permission, but asked him to return a brailler to the school office on the way. He did so in the order she requested; unfortunately, in fulfilling her request, he did not get to the bathroom soon enough. His inability to assert himself to meet his own needs or to make decisions in terms of priorities was particularly obvious that day. A sighted child has some control over his environment and inter-personal relationships because vision makes possible both a testing and imitation of adaptive actions and independent exploration of the environment. To this extent his behavior development is intrinsically motivated and not guided from without (McGuire & Meyers, 1971). In contrast, the blind child's development depends to a much greater extent upon guidance from without. This guidance comes from parents and teachers who frequently are anxious, protective, and actively supervising. The result is that the child does not learn to control his own time or to function without guidance.

□ The diagnosis of blindness or severe visual handicap in infancy is more than a medical diagnosis. The nature of congenital blindness or severe visual handicap is such that it influences every factor of the child's development. The change from babbling and sound imitation to communication, the first response to sound by reaching, the first step taken—all are bound together in such a way as to create a task unique to the congenitally blind or severely visually handicapped infant. This child faces the same developmental tasks as the sighted child; however, the route he will take to achieve them is necessarily much different. Likewise, as this child faces the developmental tasks of each succeeding stage, his resolution of them will be influenced by the particular variations inherent in them due to his visual handicap and on the success with which the previous tasks have been met. The child faces new crises in each developmental stage. This factor means that he also is a potential crisis-inducing element in the family. That is, his needs (physical, emotional, or cognitive) may be so great or so demanding or appear so overwhelming when combined with the other elements of the current family situation that a crisis arises affecting the entire family.

The Developmental Tasks

□ To summarize briefly, the family with a handicapped child has many special problems to face. For the family of a blind or severely visually handicapped child there are problems unique to them because of the cultural concepts of blindness, the frequent complications of additional impairments, and the problems inherent in each developmental stage because of the absence or impairment of vision.

Summary

Counseling services for these families can do much to replace feelings of rejection and despair with hope, as mentioned above. The counselor for a family with a blind or severely visually handicapped child must be aware of the unique needs of this child as well as those common to all children. His task is to help the family discover how they can best care for this child, to provide information concerning ways to meet his needs for supplementary stimulation, where to find people and agencies who are prepared to help them and their child, and to provide consultation to others in the community who are also working with the family and child. The fact is, however, that all too frequently counseling is not available. The medical personnel who are the first to have contact with the family frequently do not recognize the need or do not know where the family can obtain adequate counseling. Social agencies set up to serve blind persons have as their primary charge the provision of rehabilitative services aimed at preparation for employment. Professionals in family and children's agencies, mental health clinics, etc., are not

The role of the counselor

Counseling seldom available

familiar with the particular needs and unique problems of the young blind or severely visually handicapped child and his family. The one positive development in this area is that some of the public schools are extending their area of concern to the pre-school child and providing services to children from the age of three; their goal is to have the child ready for school when he reaches school age. This service has included instruction in the development of self-help skills at home and consultation to programs such as Headstart; such programs can include the blind or severely visually handicapped child when such consultation has been available.

This still leaves, however, the period from birth to three years, a period when the child must surmount many developmental difficulties if he is to be ready to develop self-help skills and then go on to formal education without handicaps in addition to his visual one. The task of the parents and child is enormous. Is it not our responsibility to see that help is available should they choose to use it?

Still neglected in the earliest years

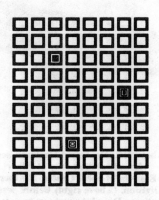

The Triumph Of David Hartman, M.D.
AMERICA'S BLIND PHYSICIAN
Class Of '76

BY ADELAIDE P. FARAH

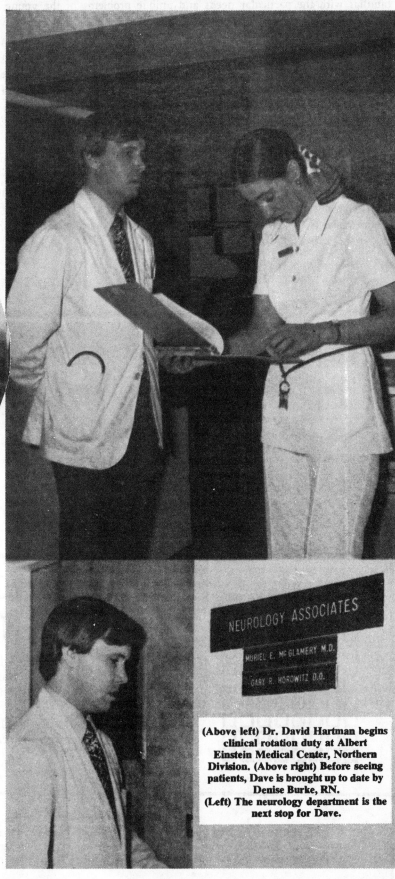

(Above left) Dr. David Hartman begins clinical rotation duty at Albert Einstein Medical Center, Northern Division. (Above right) Before seeing patients, Dave is brought up to date by Denise Burke, RN.
(Left) The neurology department is the next stop for Dave.

When Dr. David Hartman, intern in rehabilitative medicine and psychiatry, walks through Temple University Medical Center in Philadelphia, his long, collapsible metal cane precedes him. As he makes rounds, a nurse reads patient charts aloud to him. Yet for 26-year-old Dr. Hartman, who on May 27, 1976, became the first blind student in this century to graduate from medical school, blindness is less a handicap than an interesting difference.

"Now," he says reassuringly to a woman outpatient, startled at having her general physical examination conducted by a sightless doctor, "I am going to listen to your eyes!" He also listens to necks and skulls and makes diagnoses using his acute sense of touch. Graduating in the top fifth of his medical school class, he is highly regarded by his professional supervisors. Says neurologist Dr. Arnold A. Bank, "Dave gets through on merit, not because we think he's a hero!"

"America's Blind Physician," Adelaide P. Farah, *Family Health Magazine*, Vol. VIII, No. 7, July 1976. Family Communications, Inc.

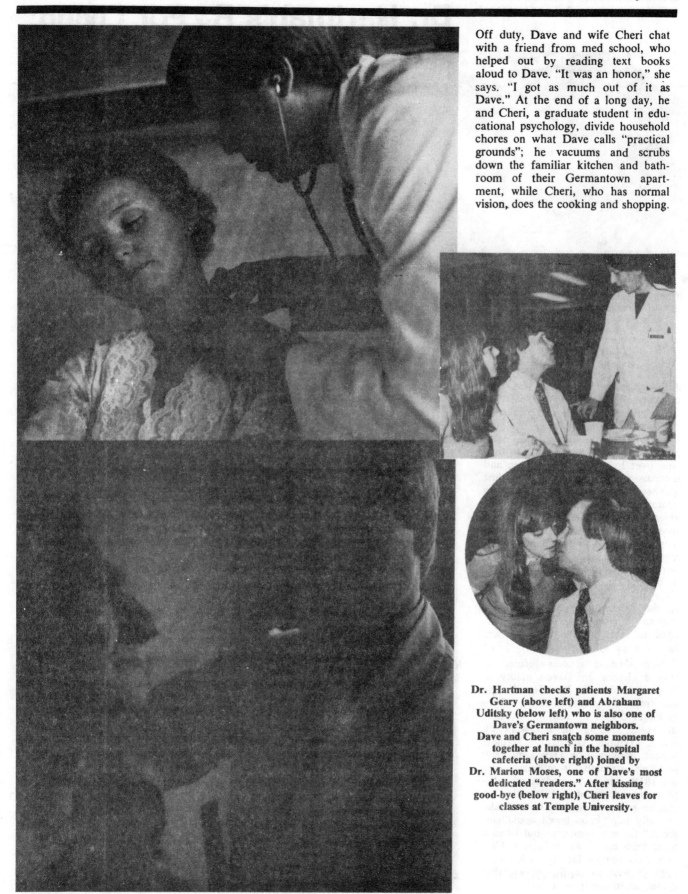

Off duty, Dave and wife Cheri chat with a friend from med school, who helped out by reading text books aloud to Dave. "It was an honor," she says. "I got as much out of it as Dave." At the end of a long day, he and Cheri, a graduate student in educational psychology, divide household chores on what Dave calls "practical grounds"; he vacuums and scrubs down the familiar kitchen and bathroom of their Germantown apartment, while Cheri, who has normal vision, does the cooking and shopping.

Dr. Hartman checks patients Margaret Geary (above left) and Abraham Uditsky (below left) who is also one of Dave's Germantown neighbors. Dave and Cheri snatch some moments together at lunch in the hospital cafeteria (above right) joined by Dr. Marion Moses, one of Dave's most dedicated "readers." After kissing good-bye (below right), Cheri leaves for classes at Temple University.

Dr. Hartman's R$_X$ For Living:

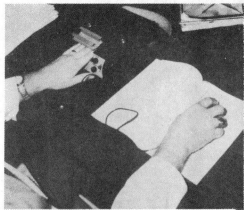

(Left) David reads charts, graphs, and EKG's on his Optacon, which translates images into vibrations. (Right) In a Temple Medical Center lab, only reading x-rays is impossible.

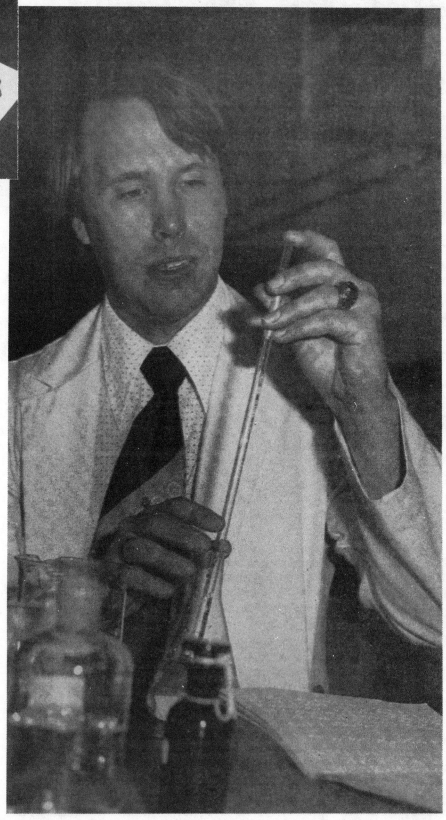

Although special instruments and techniques make some research possible, Dave prefers the risk and challenge of working with patients—like the irate woman who demanded, "What good can *you* do *me*?" and was then won over by Dave's competence and compassion. "I don't want to be just another doctor," Dave says. "I want to demonstrate to the world that a disabled person is not essentially different from anyone else. Of course we need help, but it has to be given without smothering our pride or destroying our self-reliance. I'm especially interested in helping the medical profession become more sensitive to the disabled, to the helplessness and dependency that can develop if we're not encouraged to feel valuable and to learn how to cope with the world."

Nine medical schools refused to take a chance on Dave's ability to "cope"—despite his Phi Beta Kappa key from Gettysburg College, where he majored with astonishing brilliance in biology, doing his lab work by touch. Temple University Medical School, impressed by Dave's maturity and "ego strength," admitted him as the 181st student in a class of 180—to avoid accusations of "wasting" a seat on someone unlikely to graduate. "I really didn't know how I would handle it," Dave remembers, "but I had a basic faith that I would, and I think they [the Temple faculty] did, too. I think we were pleasantly surprised that it went as smoothly as it did."

Tender, Dedicated Care

Dave and Cheri met when both were undergraduates at Gettysburg College; their romance was encouraged by Dave's parents, Mr. and Mrs. Fred W. Hartman of Havertown, Pa., who often visit them, as do many friends. The Hartmans entertain with small dinner parties, and go to movies, basketball and ice-hockey games, though Dave rarely has time to participate in his favorite undergrad sports, wrestling, weight-lifting, and cross-country running. He has never lost his sense of humor, and his frequent, appealing chuckle can be heard as he imagines improbable scenarios for his future medical career: patients shrieking and hiding as Dr. Hartman approaches with a needle to draw blood; or Dr. Hartman in surgery, ready to operate with a magic wand. Although Dave is not convinced that it is impossible for a blind doctor to be a surgeon, he has other plans.

(Above) In consultation with Dr. Arnold A. Bank, chairman of Einstein Northern's neurology department.
(Center) With med school friends George and Eileen Goldman and Buddy McManus, who call the Hartmans' apartment "our center of activity."
(Below) Idamae and Fred Hartman plan summer weekends at their New Jersey shore cottage with Dave and Cheri. Dave is an excellent swimmer.

Remembering Things Past...

Dave Hartman's desire for a career combining individual psychiatry, family therapy, and rehabilitative medicine for disabled or chronically ill people, reflects his own strong need to be treated not as a blind patient but as a whole person. His family met this need, after a shaky start.

"It was one year before Dave could accept his blindness, but it took three years and a lot of praying before his mother and I adjusted," says Dave's banker father, remembering the traumatic months after his son went blind from glaucoma and detached retinas at the age of eight. Gradually, family members fell into various complementary roles, producing what Dave calls "a team effort" to keep him from suffering psychological damage.

His mother became the person to whom Dave turned for comfort. "I would go to her and say, 'Mom, I'm sick of it all!' and come away reassured that I was still loved." When Dave ran into practical difficulties and was tempted to give up a dream because "a blind person can't do that," his father invariably put the problem into perspective: "Now, how can we arrange things so you *can* do it?" And Dave's older sister Bobbie made sure Dave was not overprotected. Idamae Hartman still remembers with rueful pride the day a neighbor asked to see Dave's first Braille watch with its touchable dial. "Bobbie will get it," said Idamae. "Dave can get it himself," said Bobbie, not budging an inch. Dave got the watch; Idamae got the message.

So successful was this "team effort" that after five years at the Overbrook School for the Blind in Philadelphia, Dave was able to attend public junior high and high schools, before entering Gettysburg College in 1968 and going on to medical school four years later.

Under the circumstances, it is not surprising that Dave fully expected to make a happy, normal marriage—or that he and Cheri plan to start a family soon after she gets her PhD. His most important goal in life—that of serving as trailblazer for other handicapped people seeking careers in medicine—may be more difficult to achieve. Those who have followed his work carefully, like Dr. M. Prince Brigham, associate dean of student affairs and admissions at Temple University Medical School, regard Dave Hartman as "a unique person" who can triumph where other handicapped aspirants might fail. But Dave is sure his example can and will be followed. "I don't think anyone knows a blind or disabled person's limitations," he says. "There is no way a sighted person can tell me what I can or cannot do."

His career thus far is eloquent testimony to that fact.

Freeing
A Bird

Emerging Trends in Rehabilitative Services

In recent years, a vast amount of innovative developments in the provision of rehabilitative services for the visually handicapped have taken place. The child with a visual impairment, through the implementation of modern technological aids to learning, may now follow a near-to-normal progression of education. Likewise, the adult affected by a visual handicap today may persue the vocational direction of his/her choice.

Specialized materials and equipment incorporated into the classroom environment, are largely responsible for these educational improvements. Improved artificial illumination has provided the visually impaired student an important variable in their learning success. Based on the fact that the visually impaired child learns a great deal aurally, the use of auditorially oriented instructional aids are necessary. The use of dictaphones, phonographs and tape recorders aids the student in areas he/she would otherwise rely on reading materials for instruction. One audio aid in particular, the talking book, has greatly increased the educational potential of the visually handicapped. These long-playing phonograph records of books read by professional readers are heard at the rate of 160-170 words per minute for fiction and approximately 150 words per minute for texts. Fortunately, the Talking Books have become standard educational media for imparting information to the visually handicapped and blind population, in both educational and vocational settings.

The current advances in services are not limited to the classroom. Adults affected by visual handicaps may equally benefit, as the occupational opportunities become more available to them.

New Devices to Help the Blind and Near-Blind

Lawrence Galton

Anna Bauer, 6, reads with help of an Optacon. The tiny camera in her right hand converts print to impulses; left hand feels letters via vibrating rods.

In a Philadelphia suburb, a blind man today gets around as he never could before—with the aid of a laser cane that probes the environment for him.

Resembling an ordinary cane, the device, with its three built-in lasers, sends out thin beams of light that not only tell him when there's an obstacle directly ahead—they warn him with auditory and tactile signals when he's approaching a dropoff such as a curb or down stairway and also when he is nearing a low-hanging tree branch, awning or sign. When the cane is silent, he knows there is an open path he can safely travel.

Daily now in Chicago, a blind World War II veteran uses his laser cane—it weighs only one pound—to go from the end of the city where he lives to the end where he works as an X-ray dark-room technician. He has to take the elevated train and two buses. "For the first time," says his wife, "I feel at peace when he leaves home."

Now mass-produced

The result of 25 years of Veterans Administration-sponsored development by Bionic Instruments, a Bala Cynwyd, Pa., bioengineering firm, the laser cane now is being produced in quantity. Its cost is $1950. Thirty to 40 hours of training in its use over a period of two weeks are needed. The Mobility Foundation of North Wales, Pa., has been formed with the primary objective of providing laser canes for those who need, want and are not financially able to purchase them.

The cane is one of a series of developments that promise to improve the lives and opportunities of many of the blind and the near-blind.

● READING MACHINES. It's called the Optacon—for optical-to-tactile conversion. In one hand, a user holds a miniature camera about the size of a small pocketknife to read printed material and convert it into impulses. And with the index finger of his other hand, the user can feel the letters and numbers via a 1" x ½" tactile array of 144 miniature vibrating rods contained in a portable, battery-operated electronics section about the size and weight of a portable cassette tape recorder. For example, as the camera moves across an "E," the user feels a vertical line and three horizontal lines moving beneath the finger.

Selling for $2895, the Optacon was developed with federal aid by a team

 New Devices to Help the Blind and Near Blind, Lawrence Galton, *Parade Magazine*, April 17, 1977. ©1977 Parade Magazine.

headed by Dr. James D. Bliss of Telesensory Systems, Inc., Palo Alto, Cal., which now produces it, and Dr. John G. Linvill of Stanford University, whose own blind daughter has also been involved in the project since 1964.

As of now, more than 3200 of the machines have been produced. With the ability to read print directly, their users can independently carry out many everyday tasks—reading their letters, bank statements and bills, following cookbook recipes, and enjoying books and magazines.

And many users have been helped to advance in jobs and enter vocations previously closed to them. Various accessories increase the Optacon's occupational usefulness. For example, accessory lenses allow a blind computer programmer to read displays on a computer video terminal and a blind secretary to read what she is typing, make corrections, and fill out preprinted forms.

Soon it will talk

The Optacon in its present form is hardly the last word. Its top reading speed now is 80 to 90 words a minute. But well within the next five years, it's expected, new accessory equipment will let the machine speak out in words and phrases, making reading speeds of up to 200 words a minute possible. And, in fact, the text-to-speech technology is well along in development by Dr. Jonathan Allen at the Massachusetts Institute of Technology.

Meanwhile, a machine that reads aloud to the blind has been developed by a brilliant, 28-year-old inventor, Raymond Kurzweil, president of Kurzweil Computer Products in Cambridge, Mass. It consists of a reading unit that resembles a tabletop copying device and a small keyboard.

When a user places a printed page

The laser cane improves mobility of the blind by using thin beams of light to probe environment ahead. Auditory and tactile signals warn of obstacles, stairs, curbs.

face down on the unit's glass top, a camera scans it line by line, converting light into electronic signals much like a photocopier. A miniature computer groups letters into words, determines

how they should be pronounced according to a preset program, then produces speech sounds, enunciating words into sentences with stresses and pauses in a metallic but understandable voice at a rate of about 150 words a minute. At the push of a button, the user can repeat or skip passages, or mark a point on the page he wants to come back to later.

Half a dozen of the machines have been built for practical testing—with promising results—in the Perkins School for the Blind, West Virginia Rehabilitation Center, Boston school system and elsewhere. At this stage, the cost of a machine is $50,000. But, with further development and volume production, it's expected to sell for about $5000 within a few years and eventually to be as portable as a briefcase.

● *TALKING CALCULATOR.* In 1976, a hand-held, battery-powered calculator that talks was chosen as one of the most significant new products of the year by Industrial Research magazine.

Called Speech Plus and developed by Telesensory Systems, makers of the Optacon, the $395 machine, weighing 17 ounces and measuring $1^1/_2'' \times 4^1/_2'' \times 7''$, can add, subtract, multiply, divide, subtotal, do square root and percentage calculations. Its numeric keys are arranged like a push-button phone because the blind are more familiar with this configuration. And the device lets the operator hear every key he presses in a clear machine voice so he knows he is making no mistakes as he goes along.

● *ELECTRONIC EYES.* Two systems now under development could hold even greater promise for the sightless.

At the Smith-Kettlewell Institute of Visual Sciences, Pacific Medical Center,

Cross-vision glasses give full vision to people blind in one eye. A pair is now worn by Israel's Gen. Moshe Dayan.

San Francisco, Dr. Paul Bachy-Rita and a research team are working with a Tactile Vision Substitution System (TVSS).

TVSS uses a tiny, battery-powered TV camera worn in the frame of a pair of glasses which picks up images, serving much like the normal lens of the eye. The camera transmits visual images to an elastic garment that fits over the abdomen and has sewn into it more than 1000 tiny electrodes. As images from the camera, translated into electrical impulses, activate the electrodes, the wearer feels vibrations on his skin in the pattern of the original images; so the skin, in effect, serves somewhat in the same way as the retina of the eye.

Objects recognized

Wearers of the experimental system have quickly learned to recognize drinking glasses, telephones and other common objects and to wend their way through tables, chairs and other obstructions in a room. A blind psychologist at the institute can move around obstacles at the rate of two feet a second, far faster than with a cane.

The institute team also developed a similar stationary system in which the camera is attached to a microscope and, instead of wearing an electrode pack, the user presses his abdomen against a bench-mounted electrode array. Using the system, one man is able to assemble small components at an electronics plant as quickly and accurately as sighted workers.

The stationary system may become available for wide use within a year or two; the portable system, still being refined, may become available a few years after that.

In an entirely different approach, Dr. William Dobelle and a research team at the University of Utah's Institute for

Biomedical Engineering are working toward a system which only a few years ago would have seemed inconceivable: one that would stimulate visual centers in the brain to let the blind see.

In experiments with a 33-year-old volunteer, blind from a gunshot accident, they have implanted a plastic strip with an array of electrodes against the visual cortex at the rear of the brain, with wires emerging through the skin above and behind an ear.

As electrical signals reach the electrodes, they're seen as spots of light, or phosphenes. In one experiment—with electrodes connected to a TV camera which sent images to a computer to be simplified and then transmitted as electrical impulses—the volunteer could see horizontal and vertical lines in the pattern of phosphenes. In another experiment, with the system hooked up to transmit Braille images, he could read words in phosphene form five times faster than with his fingertips.

Dobelle and his colleagues foresee a miniature system that the blind could wear and use constantly. It would consist of a small camera implanted in an eye socket. The camera would transmit light electronically to a tiny computer built into an eyeglass frame which would, in turn, translate the light into electrical impulses to be sent to the implanted electrodes in the visual cortex. With such a system, a wearer could perceive people and objects as well as read.

● *HELP FOR THE NEARLY BLIND.* In addition to the totally blind, half a million Americans are legally blind, with 20/200 visual acuity or with normal acuity but field of vision sharply restricted to 20 degrees or less.

Effective new devices to help them are coming out of laboratories—in particular, from the nonprofit National Institute for Rehabilitation Engineering (NIRE) in Pompton Lakes, N.J. There, a team of ophthalmologists, optometrists and engineers develops means for individual patients to make best use of their remaining sight.

Corrects tunnel vision

Not long ago, a 42-year-old man was referred to NIRE because an eye disease, retinitis pigmentosa, had left him with tunnel vision so severe that he retained only two degrees of the normal visual field, causing him to bump into objects and restricting his activities. The institute's staff designed and built for him "field expander glasses" mounted on a conventional eyeglass frame. By looking alternately through the regular lens and the field expander, he can now see a full 180 degrees. The field expander glasses now offer full-field vision, too, for people blind in one eye or with half-vision in each eye as the result of brain injury or stroke.

At NIRE, special wide-angle magnifying telescopic spectacles in bifocal form are made for people with impaired central vision or poor visual sharpness, enabling them to see clearly at a distance and drive a car again.

Strong reading spectacles with long working distances are made to help people who have been able to read only by holding print to the face. With the spectacles, they can read at a comfortable distance of 10 to 14 inches.

Miniaturized electronic devices that can be held in the hand or worn on the head are helping people unable to see adequately in dim light.

Among the remarkable achievements of NIRE are cross-vision glasses for people blind in one eye. Through technical legerdemain, the glasses provide full-field, high-acuity vision by detecting images on the blind side and conveying them to the brain through the normal optic pathways on the sighted side without causing double vision or confusion. One of those wearing the glasses is Israel's Gen. Moshe Dayan, who never expected to regain the ability to see on his left side.

Nothing can ever take the place of the priceless gift of normal sight. But increasingly now technological developments promise to help many of the partly sighted and the totally blind to gain, literally, a new outlook on the world.

Making contact

David R. Zimmerman

Shortly after the November elections, two Americans who had been very much in the national limelight visited their optometrists.

President-elect Jimmy Carter stopped in at the Brunswick, Ga., office of Dr. Carlton Hicks, who fitted him, for the first time, with one contact lens—for his right eye.

A few weeks later, TV newscaster Barbara Walters, who has worn contact lenses for years, was at the Manhattan office of Dr. Robert J. Morrison for her regular twice-annual checkup.

Jimmy Carter and Barbara Walters have different visual problems. According to Dr. Hicks, President Carter, who has not needed corrective lenses, is beginning to have difficulty in close-up reading and vision—a condition called presbyopia—which afflicts most people when they reach middle age. The TV newswoman, according to Dr. Morrison, is nearsighted, or myopic, and has trouble seeing distant objects.

Carter and Walters are among several million Americans who are beneficiaries of a major—and ongoing—revolution in contact-lens technology. They are fitted with the new, limp, water-absorbent soft contact lenses, which are much more comfortable, but also much more costly and inconvenient, than the older hard contact lenses, made of rigid material, that have been available since the 40's.

A half-dozen different soft lenses have been approved by the Federal Food and Drug Administration, and manufacturers are engaged in a fiercely competitive research and development race to bring out ever-better soft, hard and in-between lenses. The contact-lens industry believes it can capture an ever-increasing share of the market of more than 100 million Americans who now wear glasses or other corrective lenses.

A startling new advance that still is classified "experimental" in the United States could measurably contribute to this goal: The development of a lens that perhaps can be safely worn for weeks, months or even years at a time without ever being removed from the eye.

About 1.5 million Americans are fitted with contact lenses each year. The principal motive, lens fitters say, is vanity. Better vision is another. For many sports activities, contact lenses are far safer than glasses, and there are football coaches who require their weak-eyed players to wear them.

For all wearers there is the benefit, noted recently by Dr. Morrison, of coming out from behind the "vision barrier" imposed by the frames and broken visual fields of glasses. Dr. Morrison recalls one patient, a psychiatrist, who remarked that "he had lived behind glasses for so long that contacts suddenly gave him the feeling of being 'free.'"

More and more males are wearing contact lenses, although women and girls still predominate among wearers, according to one recent survey of contact-lens fitters. More than a third of wearers are students, this survey shows, with clerical workers and housewives the next two most common occupational groups, followed by professionals, laborers and teachers.

The lenses are particularly popular with entertainers and other celebrities who live in the public eye.

Not everyone who wears glasses can switch to contact lenses, however. Even Dr. Morrison—who once predicted that contact lenses would render eyeglasses obsolete—concedes that, at least for now, there are some people who cannot use them. The strong prisms that some persons need cannot be provided in contact lenses.

Common refractive, or visual, errors that contact lenses will correct include farsightedness and astigmatism; the visual distortion in astigmatism results from irregular curves on the corneal surfaces. Nearsightedness, Barbara Walters' problem, is the commonest reason for fitting contact lenses. She has been Dr. Morrison's patient for many years. For a while she wore hard lenses, but several years ago, he switched her to a new soft lens that he himself developed. He says that with contact lenses her vision now is 20/20 in each eye.

The reading problem that bothers President Carter is not always treated with contact lenses. Many middle-aged persons whose sight is otherwise normal simply get reading glasses. If they already are wearing glasses, they get bifocal lenses, in which distant vision is corrected through the central portion of the lens, while an insert at the bottom provides presbyopic correction when the wearer looks down to read. In recent years, bifocal contact lenses have been developed, but are not yet perfected. The center of the lens corrects distant vision, while the outer edge is formulated for reading.

In President Carter's case, says Dr. Hicks, the presbyopia is not severe, and may only bother the President late in the day, when he is tired. Dr. Hicks therefore will leave the President's dominant, or sharper, left eye uncorrected, for distant vision. He will try to strengthen Carter's non-dominant right eye with a soft contact lens, to make it the lead eye for reading and other close-up work.

A distinction must be made between the large majority of contact-lens wearers who have refractive errors that can be adequately corrected either with contact lenses or with glasses, and the medically more important minority for whom contact lenses may be the only way to treat severe, even blinding, eye disabilities.

The most severe of these problems is keratoconus, a disease in which the normally rounded cornea becomes progressively more conical in shape, ending vision in the eye. Patients whose eyes lack lenses are the other principal medical beneficiaries of contact lenses. This condition, called aphakia, often is produced deliberately, when eye surgeons remove lenses that have become clouded by cataracts, usually in old age. The thick spectacles that may be prescribed provide a narrow, tunnel vision—rudimentary sight at best. Contact lenses restore a full visual field.

Anyone who wants to wear contact lenses must master—and practice—the tricky maneuver of inserting the lenses. The eyelids are spread wide apart with the

Making Contact, David R. Zimmerman, *The New York Times Magazine*, February 20, 1977. ©1977 The New York Times Company.

fingertips of one hand while the opposite index finger puts the lens on the eye. Each lens is removed by putting a finger on the outside corner of the eyelids and pulling back toward the ear. A lid will catch the corner of the lens, breaking the suction, and the lens will fall out.

Many would-be wearers simply cannot put the lenses in themselves. Some of the very best candidates—elderly patients whose cataracts have been removed, for example— are disqualified because their aged hands tremble too much to manipulate the tiny lenses.

The contact lens wearer must also undergo a "break-in period." Hard-lens wearers begin by wearing their lenses an hour or less a day, gradually increasing—over weeks or even months—the length of time the lenses are worn continuously each day.

For soft-lens wearers, the break-in period may take no more than a week or so, and some wearers go almost at once to all-day wear. One New Jersey teen-ager, who disliked hard lenses because "you always feel there's something under your eyelid," says when she switched to soft lenses, "I put them in, and by the end of the day I didn't realize that they were there at all."

□

About 6 million Americans are wearing contact lenses. Half of all those who are fitted for contact lenses each year get soft lenses. First developed in Czechoslovakia in the 60's, soft lenses were brought to this country by Dr. Morrison, becoming available here in the early 70's.

If fitted properly—and this is a critical *if*—a soft lens hugs the corneal contours more closely than a hard lens can. This helps keep dust specks from slipping in between eye and lens, a common mishap with hard lenses that can cause excruciating pain. It also means that soft lenses, which cover a slightly larger portion of the eye surface than hard lenses, are less likely to pop out inopportunely. Surprisingly, though, their

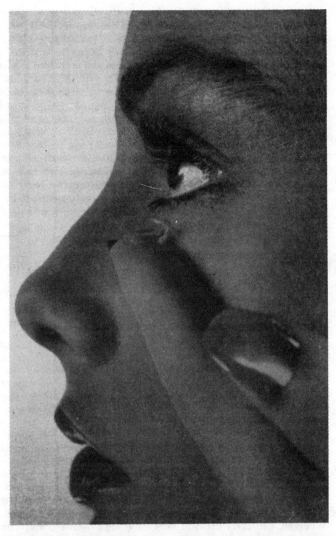

softness and pliancy may not be the principal reasons for the soft lenses' comfort. Dr. G. Peter Halberg, a Manhattan eye surgeon who is president of the Contact Lens Association of Ophthalmologists, a professional group, believes that the physical trait that helps make the lenses pliant also contributes directly to their comfort: Soft lenses are hydrophilic, or water-absorbent. They can absorb up to half or more of their weight in body-warmed tear fluid from the eye. "The soft sensation," says Dr. Halberg, "comes from the fact that the material is capable of giving off water from both sides of the lens, and is warm. Something that is wet and warm is accepted by the adjacent tissue as something akin to itself."

The key to the soft lenses' comfort is also its principal problem. The moist, warm interior of the lens is an ideal nursery for colonies of bacteria, fungi and other microorganisms that can damage the eye. As a result, soft lenses must be carefully sterilized —usually by boiling them— every day. Since eye infections can be extremely dangerous, the F.D.A. has moved with great caution in licensing lens sterilization procedures. Last year, after stubbornly resisting manufacturers' pressure for quick approval, the F.D.A. satisfied itself that a cold cleansing method—in which the lenses are soaked in solutions that kill germs and break down protein deposits from the eyes —is safe and effective—and approved it.

The soft lenses are more fragile than hard ones; they can be torn irreparably by a fingernail. Their average life span is a year to a year and a half, far less than that of hard lenses. Soft lenses also are more expensive than hard lenses. In New York City, lenses and fitting—which may require a half-dozen visits to the ophthalmologist or optometrist—can cost $300 to $500, or more.

Some soft-lens wearers say they see better with their contacts than they ever did before. But, by and large, soft lenses do not yield the clarity of vision obtainable with hard lenses. The result is that while lack of *comfort* is the principal reason why wearers abandon hard lenses, as half of them eventually do, the great majority who give up on soft ones do so because they are dissatisfied with what they can see.

For these reasons, contact-lens wearers and fitters have by no means abandoned hard lenses. Many believe that people who can comfortably wear hard lenses should do so. Dr. Halberg, who is a developer of soft lenses, says: "My first preference, if a person can wear them, is hard lenses, because of their great practicality."

☐

What promises to be the next major revolution in contact-lens technology appears to be the development of long-wearing lenses. These lenses are not yet approved by the F.D.A. and in this country are worn on an experimental basis. The F.D.A., along with leaders in the field like Drs. Halberg and Morrison, is dismayed by the rush to what it cautiously calls extended-wear lenses. The agency says the long-term safety of these lenses has not been proved.

An extended-wear lens must solve some basic physiological problems that are encountered when foreign matter is introduced onto the living tissue of the eye. Like all body tissue, the cornea must take up oxygen, cast off carbon dioxide, and dissipate into the air the heat produced in its normal metabolic activities. Corneal asphyxiation will produce redness, swelling and great pain, all of which are well known to wearers of conventional contact lenses.

Several methods to overcome these problems have been incorporated into experimental lenses that are being used for extended wear. One such lens is made of a hard, cellulose-acetate material that, its manufacturers claim, can carry off heat very well, and is permeable to both oxygen and carbon dioxide. Favorable reports on this "gas-permeable" lens have begun to appear in the medical literature. After a dozen of his patients had worn the lenses continuously for periods of six to 15 months, Dr. George E. Garcia, a Harvard ophthalmologist, judged them to be midway in comfort between conventional hard lenses and soft lenses. He said on the basis of this limited initial experience that the lenses seemed safe, and he rated them "a significant advance in the contact-lens field."

This view is shared by William McGuire, a 47-year-old contact lens technician from Cleveland, Ohio, who had himself fitted with gas-permeable lenses, and began wearing them continuously on Labor Day of 1973. Except to clean some wind-blown dust out of his eye on one or two occasions, he has not removed the lenses in the almost 1,200 days since.

If the gas-permeable lens and similar experimental new lenses pass the rigorous tests that the F.D.A. is formulating to insure that long use does not insidiously injure the eye, then extended—or even continuous—wear may be the next contact-lens trend.

Katie's Eyes Are Normal Now

A father's moving account
of his three-year-old daughter's bravery,
and his own fears, as she underwent
two operations on her eyes.

by ERIC LARSEN

■ The doctor assured us that this type of eye surgery
was not dangerous. "But when you are dealing with
the eyes," he said, "there is always risk." He didn't
condescend to us; he knew we preferred the truth.

"There is no such thing as routine surgery of the
eye," he went on. "But I can assure you that this
type is extremely common." He gave us the statistics.
"Two out of every 100 children are affected by
the problem. One out of every 100 is severe enough
to require surgery. Of these, 60 to 65 percent can be
corrected with a single operation."

Carolyn and I were in his office, sitting on chairs
pulled up to his desk. Behind us through the open
door I could see Katie, alone in the waiting room,
sitting on a blue sofa slowly turning the pages of
a children's book. With the drops in her eyes I
doubted that the pictures looked like anything but a
blur, but even so she turned the pages slowly,
pretending to study each one in detail, as if nothing
were out of the ordinary. Clinging to safety. All
over again I was struck by the dignity and bravery
of a three-year-old child who is badly frightened.
Sitting in the examination chair, Katie had not cried
once, except when the doctor put in the drops, and
then only for a moment. She gripped Carolyn's hand,
who sat on a straight chair beside her. "Mommy,
now I can't see you," she said in a voice so small
as to be almost inaudible. She was scared.

"And the other 35 percent?" It was Carolyn
questioning the doctor, her own voice somewhat
hushed with apprehension and fear.

"Almost 100 percent are correctable with a second
operation," the doctor said.

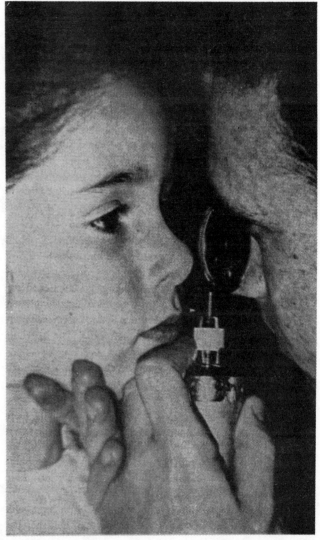

PHOTO MEDIA

That night in bed we talked late. "Poor Katie,"
Carolyn kept saying, "what awful luck she has." She
wept for a few minutes, leaning her face against
me. Carolyn was four months pregnant, and she was
suddenly filled with fears for the second baby, as well.

"He's a good doctor," I told her, feeling the
weakness of my words. I put my arms around her.
"And Katie will be lucky. We all will."

The next day I found Carolyn at the kitchen
table, poring over the dictionary.

4. EMERGING TRENDS

"Did you know it comes from the Greek word for squinting?" Carolyn said, forcing her tone, making it sound clinical and brave. "Here." She read to me. "Strabismus, the inability of one eye to attain binocular vision with the other because of imbalance of the muscles of the eyeball." Then she paused. "Only with poor Katie it's both of them."

I stood behind Carolyn and put my hands on her shoulders, feeling again as if there were nothing I could do. Only six weeks earlier we had first noticed it, Katie closing one eye when she looked at us because the other one rolled outward, out of her control.

In the hospital, Carolyn slept on a cot alongside Katie's bed. The worst part was when Katie came out of the anesthetic, her eyes covered in bandages, unable to see. She was sedated and soon fell asleep again, but not before she understood that she was blinded. She clutched Carolyn's hand and whispered over and over in a tiny, terrified little voice on the edge of tears, "Mommy, I can't see you anymore. Mommy, I can't see you anymore." The operation had been early in the morning, and I went to the hospital as soon as I could get free from work that evening. Walking into the room, I was not certain for a moment how well I was going to be able to handle myself. When I see Katie, especially in new surroundings, I am often struck by how very small she still is, a tiny body that you can pick up and hold and comfort. And there she was, sleeping in the huge bed, miles too big for her, her long hair spread across the white pillow, and the whole upper part of her little face in bandages, with huge white gauze pads where her brown eyes should be. But I was powerless to pick her up and hold her, even to speak to her, or to do anything at all but look.

When the doctor removed Katie's bandages a day and a half after the surgery it was shocking to see the whites of her eyes. They were blood red, and there were dark bruises in the flesh around them. The doctor told us that it would be as long as a month before he could tell whether the operations had been successful, but at home we felt that we knew much sooner than that. One eye did seem to be corrected, but the other still turned outward, choosing its own moments to do so, roaming sideways out of Katie's control. We saw the doctor regularly, and he still hoped that the muscles might strengthen themselves, but in late September he confirmed that a second operation would be necessary for one eye.

He scheduled the surgery for the first week in November. Meanwhile Katie was to continue wearing her patch four hours a day over the good eye, still in hopes that the weak one could be strengthened by use.

We were frightened, and so was Katie, no matter how hard we tried not to let her sense our own fear. Both Carolyn and I became superstitious, saw omens in everything. The Saturday before Hallowe'en, I remember, I went out with Katie to buy a Jack O'Lantern at the vegetable market in the neighborhood. There were rows of pumpkins on display on the sidewalk, all sizes and shapes, glowing in the warm October sunlight. Katie and I surveyed them all, and at last she picked one out, a very small one, perfectly round. Then she wanted it painted.

"Daddy," she said, beckoning me with her finger to bend down so she could whisper something in my ear. I bent down and Katie, wearing her black patch, cupped her hand at my ear and whispered, "Can I have a face?"

A panel truck was parked at the curb with its side door open, and in the darkness inside a young man sat on an upended orange crate, surrounded by pots of paint with brush handles sticking out of them, painting faces on pumpkins.

"Sure," I told Katie. "Sure you can have a face." But then she beckoned me again, and I bent down, and she whispered in my ear once more.

"With a patch on it," she said.

From that point on, my anxiety increased. Katie and I stood at the door of the panel truck watching the young man inside as he worked on her small pumpkin. He was kind, doing all he could do to please us, but I realized as he began working that something was terribly wrong. In her three-year-old innocence, I think Katie saw nothing of it, but I was in agonies of regret. The young man worked with unconscionable slowness, searching endlessly for the right brushes in his semicircle of pots, slowly withdrawing them only to drop them accidentally, then feeling with his hands on the cluttered floor of the truck to find them. He dropped the pumpkin, itself (which made Katie giggle), overturned a pot of paint, picked up the pumpkin only to have it slip again from his fingers, which by now left ghoulish prints of red wherever he touched it. I had explained to him, where he sat in the shadow inside the truck, that Katie wanted a pirate's face, and when he turned to look at Katie to use her patch as a model, I saw that one of his own eyes was gray and clouded, the other turned out and squinting. Of course it was too late, there was no going back and, in a kind of horror, I waited while he fumbled with his paints, dropping the pumpkin again. He spent more time wiping away smears than in painting the face.

In the end he produced something that was spectacular in its rough disorder—a gash of a mouth, off-center nose, strange green hair, scarred cheek, huge black patch over one eye. I remember walking home, filled with superstitious dread, and carrying the ominous pumpkin on one hand like a grotesque severed head, while Katie, in one of those moments when she entirely forgot all her own fears—forgot everything about doctors, hospitals, eyedrops and patches—skipped gleefully on the sidewalk ahead of me, singing one of her private songs and dancing toward home.

I never told Carolyn the whole story. For a week, right through Katie's operation, that Jack O'Lantern sat on a windowsill in the living room, filling me with fear and pity and dread and prayers, while every now and then, Katie herself, wearing her own black patch, would come skipping gaily into the room, pat it once on the head, greet it happily, then skip back out to play in the other room. She adored it.

As it turned out, I was right in the beginning. We were all lucky. The second operation was a success. Katie's eyes are normal now. When I think back to the surgery, to Katie's bravery, to all our fears, I remember Hallowe'en and that pumpkin. I remember Katie patting it on the head, and skipping out of the room, and I think, yes how lucky we were. My God, how very lucky we are.

How to Spot Vision Problems in Young Children

An early-warning checklist from the National Society for the Prevention of Blindness to help parents safeguard their youngsters' sight.

SIGNS OF POSSIBLE EYE TROUBLE IN CHILDREN

If the following are present your child's eyes should be examined by a medical eye specialist.

BEHAVIOR

Rubs eyes excessively.

Shuts or covers one eye, tilts head or thrusts head forward.

Has difficulty in reading or in other work requiring close use of the eyes.

Blinks more than usual or is irritable when doing close work.

Holds books close to eyes.

Is unable to see distant things clearly.

Squints eyelids together or frowns.

APPEARANCE

Crossed eyes.

Red-rimmed, encrusted or swollen eyelids.

Inflamed or watery eyes.

Recurring styes.

COMPLAINTS

Eyes itch, burn or feel scratchy.

Cannot see well.

Dizziness, headaches or nausea following close eye work.

Blurred or double vision.

A BRIEF DICTIONARY OF EYE DISORDERS

AMBLYOPIA

Dimness of vision without any apparent disease of the eye. This is usually the result of not using an eye ("lazy eye") in order to avoid the discomfort of double vision caused by a muscle problem.

ASTIGMATISM

An eye problem in which there is blurred vision because of irregularities in the shape of the cornea—the transparent covering of the eye—or of the lens. Because light rays cannot focus on the retina, it is difficult to see far and near objects.

COLOR DEFICIENCY

An inherited vision defect, not a disease, characterized by the inability to distinguish colors —usually red or green but sometimes blue or yellow.

HYPEROPIA (Farsightedness)

In farsighted eyes, the eyeball is too short from front to back. Farsighted people see faraway objects well but things that are close are blurry.

MYOPIA (Nearsightedness)

In myopia, the eyeball is too long from front to back. Nearsighted people see nearby objects well but not things that are far away.

STRABISMUS (Squint, Crossed Eyes)

One or more muscles of the eye is out of balance, causing one or both eyes to turn inward or outward, making it impossible for both eyes to look at the same object at the same time.

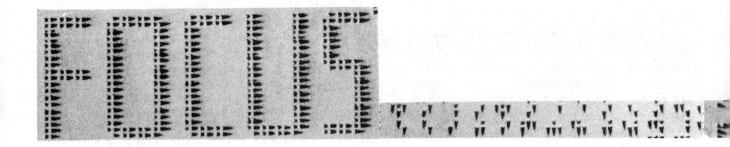

BRAILLE:

System Devised Over 100 Years Ago by Louis Braille

Louis Braille became blind at 3 years of age, but despite his handicap he acquired an education and eventually became a great teacher. He also played excellent organ. . . .

Through his own experiences with the difficulty in being blind he developed this system now used by the blind the world over.

The dots are raised — they are made with a tool that looks somewhat like an awl with a dull rounded end to keep it from perforating the special Braille paper which is thick and soft — it is held in a special frame with a metal guide which helps the blind person make the holes in a straight line.

Braille requires no more than 5 dots to make any letter. A word does not have to be completely spelled out, as certain arrangements of dots are used to represent commonly used syllables and even whole words. EXAMPLE: FOR is made of 6 dots arranged in two rows of three. Thus a blind student is able to take notes in class at a rapid pace.

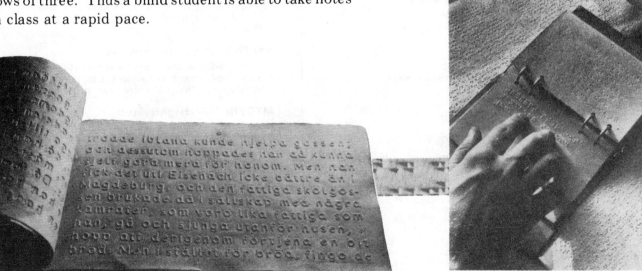

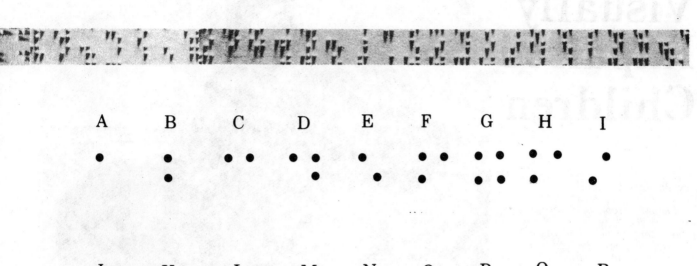

A	B	C	D	E	F	G	H	I

J	K	L	M	N	O	P	Q	R

S	T	U	V	W	X	Y	Z	'

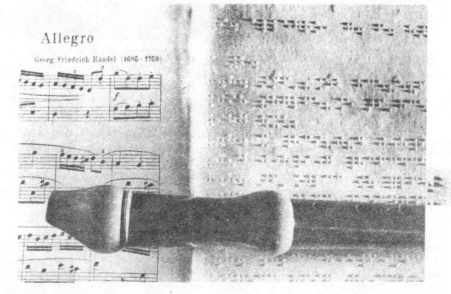

Allegro

Georg Friedrich Händel (1685 - 1759)

Foster Family Care for Visually Impaired Children

Photo: Nassau BOCES

by Pauline M. Moor

Pauline M. Moor is a former program specialist with the American Foundation for the Blind. As a New York-based free-lance consultant in the development of visually impaired children, she is working throughout the country with agencies, schools serving young children and families, and colleges and universities involved in teacher preparation.

Although he is legally blind, this 6-year-old foster child enjoys, with his teacher's help, the same simple picture books that sighted children do. . .

"But if he can't see, I don't know if I can care for him. What special things would I have to do for him?"

This is a natural question asked by parents, foster parents and others responsible for the care of a child who has severe visual impairment. At one time such doubts were considered so realistic and insurmountable that they impeded expansion of foster family services for visually impaired children. Fortunately, there is today a body of pertinent information that not only aids in understanding the needs of the child and the parents but is supportive to all caretakers of such a child, whether they are the biological, adoptive or foster parents or care for the child in a home or institutional setting.

In the early 1900s, institutional foster care for a young child with severe visual impairment was an accepted practice and frequently recommended, especially if a child was diagnosed as blind in infancy. It was a general assumption that parents who learned that their infant was blind would not have the specialized knowledge necessary for his care and that the child would benefit from being in a setting where experienced personnel could attend to his special needs. This belief gave rise to such homes as The Arthur Sunshine Home and Kindergarten for Blind Babies in New Jersey, The Boston Nursery for Blind Babies in Massachusetts, and similar institutions in England. Emphasis was generally placed upon nursing care, the rationale being that severe visual impairment was a medical problem.

These specialized institutions offered care until the child reached school age, when it was anticipated he or she would enter a residential academic school. For those children who appeared to be developing more slowly, there were the institutions for the retarded and many children with severe visual impairment were undoubtedly referred to the latter during the early part of this century. Placement of a visually impaired child in a foster family home was a comparatively rare exception.

New insights from the field of child development have led to new attitudes and policies. Today, foster family

Foster Family Care for Visually Impaired Children, Pauline M. Moor, *Children Today*, Vol. 5 No. 4, July/August 1976. ©1976 Children's Bureau, Office of Child Development.

care is often recommended but factors other than visual loss alone naturally influence such a placement decision, not the least of which should be consideration of what arrangement may lead to optimal growth and development of the child.

The child's own parents and home are generally considered to be the most desirable environment for any growing child. However, there are many circumstances that can preclude such home care, such as a family lifestyle that would not be conducive to the child's optimal development, financial problems, illness of a parent, an additional handicapping condition in the child or another member of the family, parental attitudes toward the handicap and parents' feelings of inadequacy in regard to coping with everyday living problems.

Most parents are able to provide home care for their visually impaired child, usually with some professional assistance, but many are not, especially if a severe visual loss is accompanied by other severely handicapping conditions. Children who are blind and in foster care settings today are often children with multiple impairments.

As more knowledge emerges in relation to the development of a child with a perceptual problem, in this instance a visual loss, there is greater realization that children with visual impairments are more like sighted children than they are different. They have the same growth patterns and, like sighted children, show great variation in rates of growth and development and, often, in their developmental sequences. Sometimes a child has spurts of growth; on the other hand, the increments may be so small as to be hardly noticeable—and parents wonder if their child will ever learn. The major difference is in how a child learns, how he finds and acquires information about himself, people, objects and the world around him. Based on studies of children with visual impairment and on information from parents who have shared their experiences and feelings, certain suggestions may be helpful to those who are responsible for the care of a visually impaired child in a home, school or hospital setting.

Learning About Visual Impairment

A foster parent or other caretaker should be familiar with what has caused a child's loss of sight, for the diagnosis has some implications for the amount of residual vision the child may be expected to have. Few

"blind" persons—children or adults—have no sight at all or only light perception; most persons have some residual vision.

The ophthalmologist can measure the child's visual acuity and indicate how much the child probably sees, but more significant than the numerical acuity is how the child uses any vision that he has. The person caring for the child, on the other hand, through daily observation, will usually have more information on how and what he is able to see. For example, does he turn his head in a certain direction, indicating that he sees better in this way? Does he hold objects close to his face? Sometimes a child will appear to have more vision than at other times, depending upon such factors as background area, brightness or dimness of light, color and contrasts.

Foster parents can encourage use of vision by providing toys that are colorful and involve movement, such as a mobile over a crib or carriage, and by playing games that require following a moving object, such as a toy car or a large rolling ball. Storybooks with clear pictures and a minimum of detail will help the child to "learn" to use any vision he may have.

A visual loss may result from whatever has caused other handicapping conditions, as in the instance of prenatal infection and prematurity. Though blindness has often been associated with extreme prematurity, the prematurity of the child who is blind should not be assumed to be a determinant of any additional impairment. Gross impairments are detectable at birth; however, certain perceptual problems such as a hearing or visual loss or a retardation of biogenetic origin may be more difficult to diagnose in a very young child. If a child appears to be developing more slowly than anticipated, the delay, which may be a pseudo-retardation, is usually attributable to other than prenatal or neonatal factors.

A foster parent will want to know at what age visual impairment occurred. If a school-age or older preschool-age child has lost his vision as a result of illness or accident, he or she has already acquired self-help skills and a body of knowledge about the world and people. On the other hand, the congenitally blind child must learn to walk, talk, feed and dress himself and acquire the same knowledge without the great aid of vision. He or she needs assistance

and motivation in approaching each task. There is no incentive to reach out for a bright rattle or to follow a rolling ball. A visually handicapped child does not respond to a mother's smile, unless she speaks at the same time. He may show little interest in the task of learning to feed himself, tedious without sight, unless there is a "reward" such as the enthusiastic approval or loving pat of a parent. Learning to walk unassisted requires not only a sense of balance but the courage and confidence parents can give as a child steps forward into unknown space.

Motor Development

The young child should have ample opportunity to move freely within the limits of safety. A baby is enticed to move from one position to another by a sound toy, a soft ball or rattle, and by his mother's coaxing voice. The toy itself is sufficient motivation for the sighted child, but the parent must provide the motivation for the visually impaired child. Toys may be scattered nearby on the floor so that the child will come in contact with them as he or she stretches, rolls over and creeps.

A child should be helped to be up on his feet and moving about on his own as early as possible. In this way he will learn about his surroundings and his curiosity will be whetted. As he travels about the house, climbing on the divan and going over stairs, he will be learning about distances, heights and the reverberative sounds of objects in space. He is also learning about himself and what he is able to do. He has a feeling about himself as a person. He can be the cause of an effect, rather than always being on the receiving end as objects come to him.

Short walks with his parents or caretakers to the store, through the woods or along a city street—with the child's attention called to sounds, surfaces and differing smells—will help increase awareness of his environment and enhance the development of his other sensory avenues of learning. Such learning experiences are not only important to his early development but also to his ability to move freely and to travel independently later as a youth or adult—with or without the use of a cane or guide dog.

Communication

The visually impaired child is never so isolated as when he is beyond the range of hearing those sounds that in-

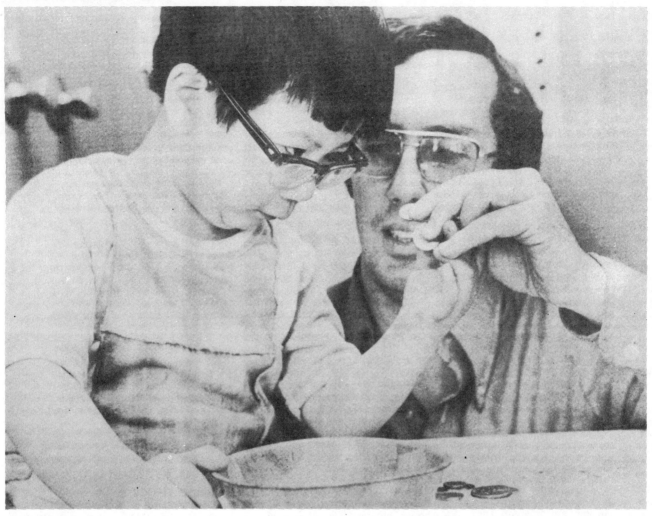

Photo: Nassau BOCES

. . .This fall he will enter kindergarten at his local public school, where an itinerant teacher from the Vision Impaired Program of the Board of Cooperative Educational Services (BOCES) of Nassau County, New York, will help him make the transition into the integrated classroom. Here, his teacher in the Nassau BOCES preschool program helps him learn to identify coins.

dicate the existence or presence of people. A baby should be kept near enough to his parent or caretaker during the day to hear her working about the home—sweeping the floor, cooking in the kitchen, washing dishes—and sufficiently close to be spoken to and so reassured of her presence.

Sometimes parents think that radio or television will serve the same purpose. However, too much auditory stimulation of this kind is undesirable, and it is no substitute for the presence of people and the development of relationships.

Talking to a child and playing simple lap games such as "Clap your hands," "Put your fingers on your toes" and "Peek-a-boo" are ways in which a child can become familiar with the adult, enjoy the care he is receiving and at the same time learn about his own body.

Not all communication is verbal. One quickly learns the subtle cues a child gives: those of pleasure— a smile, a gurgle, a laugh, a jump; those of resistance—turning away from the feeding spoon; and those of seeking closer contact that express the need for comfort and reassurance. One of the most meaningful forms of communication with a child is tactual—by holding, cuddling, taking his hand and assuring him that his confidence and trust in you are well placed.

A cardinal principle should be to speak to a blind child upon entering the room so that he may know who has come in. If one is addressing him where others are present, it is helpful to turn in his direction and call him by name. Children learn that voices come from different directions and they can localize sound in this way. Since a child's name is his identification, his concept of himself as a person is strengthened by its use.

In talking with a visually impaired child one should always use clear, distinct speech, describing what is taking place in as much detail as the child can absorb. Long detailed explanations are not always necessary and may only clutter the child's associations. However, it is all too easy to assume that the child has certain understandings that normally come through vision. Knowing what and when a child is comprehending is undoubtedly part of the skill of teaching any child.

Self-Help Skills

As a child reaches new levels of development in motor and language areas, he or she will also show readiness for learning certain self-help skills. Methods or strategies that have proved to be beneficial in teaching children to feed themselves, to dress and to take care of all toilet and personal needs are also used with children who have severe visual impairment. There is no one blueprint for the successful teaching of any of these skills since each child is an individual and foster parents and other caretakers have their own personalities, judgment and ways of teaching. The literature abounds with suggestions that may be useful at one time or another.

When little or no apparent progress is being made in one instance, less emphasis may be put on that particular learning activity for the time being and attention given to another area in which the child seems more ready for learning. Parents who have become discouraged over toilet training, for example, have often found that if they can forget the issue for a while the child will respond more readily at a later date. Meanwhile, the child is maturing and learning in many other areas.

It may be helpful to set a learning goal, then examine the learning tasks involved and teach each of these sequential steps separately. Prescriptive teaching and task analysis are useful strategies, particularly for children who are multiply impaired or are showing learning disabilities. Charting a child's achievements helps to identify small increments of progress. Parents and other caretakers invariably use a certain amount of task analysis as they learn to recognize the extent to which a child is capable of performing a certain task, such as climbing on a chair and turning on the faucet for a glass of water.

It should always be remembered that the child who is functioning with little or no useful vision will require more time and practice to develop any skill. Although he will need assistance at first, he may eventually discover his own way of achieving the same end, one that is more adaptable to his lack of sight. The adult should be consistent and patient, and offer encouragement and praise as the child learns each new step in the process, whether it be taking off a shoe, managing a cup and spoon or caring for his personal belongings.

Educational Services

Foster parents and other caretakers will want to know about available educational services. Although "education" and "school" are frequently synonymous in one's thinking, it is recognized that education for any child begins at birth, for every minute is a learning experience. He is learning as he plays with materials that are heavy and light, round and square, large and small. He is learning as he turns the wheels of a tricycle, or drops a letter in the mailbox. Such common childhood experiences should also be part of the early education of the child who is visually impaired.

The child should also be given opportunities to learn about the world outside of his home: the neighborhood, church, playmates and their homes. Children learn many things from other children that they can not learn from adults—sharing toys, taking turns in play, dealing with reactions of other children. Many visually impaired children attend regular playgroups, nursery schools, Head Start and other educational programs along with sighted children. When a child is ready for a group experience—and foster parents and other caretakers may seek some assistance from the Special Education Division of their local school system or the State Services for the Blind in determining his readiness—local resources should be investigated.

A child who participates in group activities with sighted children has a greater variety of experiences than can usually be offered at home. In addition to acquiring new concepts about play and people, he will begin to think of himself as being like other children as he learns more about them. They, too, are learning about him and his special needs. Recent legislation has facilitated the integration of children with disabilities into regular educational programs, though the many benefits to children who are visually impaired have been demonstrated for some time.

Even before the child is ready for an academic program, the local school system should be approached for information regarding services offered to visually impaired children. In many communities the child may be enrolled in the regular classroom of his local school, where he may receive such supplementary services as special instruction from a specially trained teacher, and have access to appropriate educational equipment. In some communities, supplementary assistance may be provided by a visiting teacher who comes regularly to the school to work with the child. .

Since education is compulsory for all children who are educable, each state is responsible for insuring that an educational program is offered to visually impaired children. Some children will attend a residential facility where services are appropriate to the child's developmental and special needs, while other visually impaired children may live in residential settings for the retarded, where increasing attention is being given to special needs because of a sensory impairment.

Assessment

It is natural for parents to have questions at one time or another concerning a child's progress, and to think that an assessment or evaluation would be useful in helping them to a better understanding of his or her development. However, one must be aware that instruments for evaluating the development of a young visually impaired child are limited both in number and in their prognostic validity. Evaluations involve careful observation and attention to significant information. For example, has the child had long hospitalizations or any traumatic and anxiety-producing experience, especially during a "critical" period of his development? One such period would be the first few weeks of life, when a baby needs tactual contact and kinisthetic as well as other sensory experiences—patting and stroking during his bath, playing with his arms and legs and, of course, talking to him so that he knows one is close to him.

The adult, at home or in the classroom, needs to have some baseline for assessing what should be expected or anticipated as far as the child's achievements are concerned. With a basic knowledge of normal child development, the adult can adapt this guide as necessary to allow for vision impairment. For example, a visually impaired child cannot be expected to develop concepts of space unless he has experiences that give him a feeling of distance and of space—a long ride, the time it takes to walk down the school corridor, reaching for bars on the jungle-gym. While there will be many adjustments, foster parents and other caretakers should try to keep their expectations high and as near to normal development as possible.

Persons who are familiar with blindness and its effects upon the development of the child are available in almost every community and can be called upon to discuss questions and problems that naturally arise as children grow and develop. In addition, the Rehabilitation Services (Division of Services to the Blind and Visually Handicapped) and State Department of Education (Division of Special Education) in every state distribute literature upon request, and many specialized agencies offer counseling services, including home visits by qualified personnel.

To meet recent legislative requirements, public school systems will be offering a variety of educational services, including not only day classes but also home visiting, especially for younger children, and referral of children with additional impairments to appropriate specialized resources for treatment or therapy. Inquiry should be made of the State Department of Education, Division of Special Education, or of the Rehabilitation Services, Services for the Blind, for information pertaining to resources in a particular community or region.

It is hoped that these suggestions will aid foster parents and other caretakers in understanding the special needs of a child with visual impairment, and help to alleviate some of their initial feelings of inadequacy in regard to caring for him. It is assumed that the child in foster family care will maintain a relationship with his own family, and that foster parents will use available medical, social and educational resources as necessary, and also maintain a close relationship with the foster care agency that facilitates the use of these resources.

While the focus here has been upon a child's special needs because of severe visual impairment, those caring for him will become increasingly aware of his likeness to all children. As the child grows and develops, foster parents particularly may look at his or her achievements as part of the return for their loving care and guidance. Emphasis will have shifted from attention to the disability to a greater appreciation of the child's many capabilities.

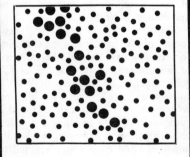

Blind Justice or Justice for the Blind: Future Directions in Civil Rights—Due Process, Equal Protection, and Statutory Law

Jonathan M. Stein

[This address was delivered in New Orleans, July 7, 1977, at the 37th Annual Convention of the NFB. Mr. Stein is Chief of Law Reform at Community Legal Services, Philadelphia.]

The 1960's constituted a great watershed in the legal development of civil rights of minority groups, of which the blind movement was and is an integral part. A watershed that is putting this country finally, and perhaps a hundred years late, on the road to making this an egalitarian society.

These legal developments from the 1960's have a number of lessons for us today as we look into the 70's and 80's. The Gurmankin case which I litigated in Philadelphia illustrates a number of these lessons for us.

As many of you know, Judy Gurmankin was a blind school teacher in Philadelphia who graduated from Temple University in 1968; and from 1968 on through the mid 1970's was completely barred from being able to teach sighted students in any public school in Philadelphia. She wasn't even allowed to take the teachers examination that the Philadelphia school system gave. developed under title VII of the 1964 Civil Rights Act, where race and sex discrimination are prohibited. There the Equal Employment Opportunity Commission (the EEOC) has developed law which even this Supreme Court—the Berger Court—can't really undermine very much. I have to say "very much" because they are doing their job to undermine it a bit. But there is still good law out there that says that remedial steps have to be taken to cure the present effects of past discrimination. That means if an employer—a private employer or a government employer—has been discriminating, it means that not only must the employer hire that individual who is complaining, but he must also set up preferences, hiring quotas, and goals to ensure that other people who are the victims of discrimination get hired at the same time. The area of remedies is something that has to be addressed and it has to be addressed in a very vigorous way.

The Gurmankin case is still going on. That's one aspect of litigation—it almost never ends. Hopefully, you can get some benefits out of it during the course of it, and I think that's what the name plaintiff—Judy Gurmankin—has gotten out of it. She is now a full-time teacher of English in the Philadelphia school system.

But she is not stopping there, and there's a lesson to learn here. She's gotten her job, and she's getting a good salary now, but she's also insisting that other things be done by this federal court to make sure that the Philadelphia school system really changes, not just changes with respect to one person in a system where 15,000 teachers are employed.

Among the things she is insisting, some of them go to her own benefit, and those include not only a job for herself but a "make whole" remedy, which is the name given to make sure that someone is "made whole" again. She could have taught in the school system in 1970, and a federal court in Philadelphia—with the court of appeals affirming—has said she has to be given six years of seniority—full seniority as if she began in 1970. We're going to insist that she be given full back pay. We're going to teach the Philadelphia school system, and hopefully, every other employer in this country, that if they're going to discriminate, they're going to have to pay for it. For [Judith Gurmankin] that means full back pay, full interest, and every other health and fringe benefit that she would have had if she had begun teaching in 1970.

But in addition to that—and this brings me back to the need for affirmative action remedies—we're going to seek an affirmative action plan for all visually handicapped teachers so that preferences, quotas, and hiring goals will be established to hire other visually handicapped teachers in the Philadelphia school system. And we're not going to settle our suit until that is achieved.

That's one aspect of full justice for the blind. Another aspect is the idea of achieving institutional and class-wide relief. This goes back to the idea that full justice is not full justice unless it goes beyond the individual who happens to have either been aware of his or her legal rights, or had the luck to find a lawyer to pursue his or her claim. This is premised on the idea that any discrimination based on one's blindness, or for that matter, on one's race, or on one's sex, is discrimination against a class of everyone who is either blind or black or a woman. Any action one takes—whether it be in the court forums or in the legislature or on the picket lines—is an action which must be taken on behalf of a class of people.

Fortunately, the courts allow classes of people to bring lawsuits. Those are called class actions. When Judy Gurmankin sued, she brought a suit on behalf of herself and on behalf of all other blind teachers similarly situated, who could teach in the Philadelphia school system. I would like to urge the folks here, when they consider filing their administrative complaints with the Labor Department (under section 503 of the Rehab Act), or HEW (under section 504 of the Rehab Act)—and these, as you may know, need only be a letter, a written letter to the regional office of Labor, or for HEW, I think their Washington Office for Civil

Rights is taking complaints under 504.

When you do file these complaints with the federal agencies, or for that matter, with a state human rights agency, you should file them as a class action so that you seek not only to benefit that named individual who has been discriminated against, but you insist that that federal or state agency take all the steps necessary to change the system-wide practices of the social agency, employer, or what have you, who has been discriminating. Because it's going to be very easy for agencies, in a sense, to buy off people by giving one person a nice settlement. In fact, federal and state agencies, given their heavy caseloads and even, I'm sure, very well-meaning people, also would feel comfortable having individuals take something away that benefits them [so the agency can move] on to the next hundred cases they have to deal with.

It's going to take a lot of courageous people who are not going to be satisfied with, simply, individual relief and will insist that agencies provide relief for a whole class of people, and that they change entire employment practices or entire procedures of how an agency deals with a class of people. In the Gurmankin case that is part of our philosophy of the case. Other blind teachers will be hired.

We have challenged the testing procedures: Philadelphia used a very biased oral examination in which two teachers in the system put applicants through an oral examination. Interestingly enough, in 1974 the school system said, Okay, we'll give Judy the teachers exam. Go away and be happy now. Now you're equal; now you can take an exam like everyone else.

But lo and behold, the discrimination which was pretty gross before—which said that no blind teacher could even take the exam—took a more subtle form in the oral exam. There the oral examiners, through a series of biased questions and subtle assumptions about the blind teacher, continued the discrimination that the total bar illustrated earlier. Another form of subtle discrimination they practiced was that they gave extra score points on the teachers exam to teachers who [had done their student-teaching] in the Philadelphia school system. But they barred blind student teachers from teaching in the school system, so that any blind teacher like Judy

Gurmankin did not get the extra seven score points which assured you of a very high position on the eligibility list. No one in the school system even saw this as discrimination; they saw it as sort of a historic occurrence that just happened.

As one pursues discrimination cases, one has to look very carefully and scrutinize every aspect of every admission requirement, every testing procedure, and the like, to ensure that they are in fact fair and job-related. That again is one thing which the 1964 Civil Rights Act and the EEOC are doing. Every employment test in the country is subject to that type of scrutiny, to ensure that every aspect of it is job-related. When there is discrimination, the burden is not on the *victim* of the discrimination to show that the test is not job-related. The *company* has to come forward—as the Supreme Court has held—to justify every aspect of that admissions or job-screening test.

What we're trying to do in this case is not only open up jobs but completely overhaul the testing procedures being used, and to make sure that, in addition, there is outreach, that there is advertising, that people are encouraged to apply to the Philadelphia school system. I would urge people here, if you know school teachers or if there are some school teachers among you, that you very definitely seek employment in the Philadelphia school system. And if you do, drop me a line or give me a call, because I'd be very interested in knowing of applicants who are applying there. We want to make sure that the right we've established is a real one and that there are real jobs that are opened up as a result of it.

Let me at this point state a few cautionary notes about the courts and lawyers. I'm part of that system, so let me be as candid as I can. The courts and lawyers have been very significant in developing legal rights. Courts do give moral legitimacy to a cause, and courts also have the power to sock it to other institutions, whether they be mayors, governors, Presidents, or legislatures. But keep in mind the following problems in the legal process and with judges and lawyers:

(1) The legal process can be a very time-consuming and costly one. Lawsuits go on and on, and the immediate benefits are not always that apparent.

(2) The system is only as good as the judges; and judges aren't the most liberal or enlightened folks around.

(3) There can be too great a reliance on lawyers and lawsuits. Where lawyers take too much of a lead, there can be too great a dependency built up on them and too much can be taken away from building an organization and from utilizing political and direct action forums which can often get you a lot more than a single judge can. Courts and lawsuits can often become antiseptic forums where things have to be orderly and too quiet, and that is not always the best means of building an organization, of getting the word to the public, and of using the political processes.

To illustrate that, the 504 regulations took a good while getting out. Although there was a lawsuit filed in D.C. to help get them out, there was nothing like sitting in the offices of Secretary Califano to finally get those 504 regulations out. I think there is a good lesson there on the limitations of the legal process in terms of getting you what you want.

Let me say a word about the access to legal services. . . . Where can you get legal services and legal help? As I say, the rights that are on the statute books don't mean a thing if you can't enforce them. The first thing—and it may be an obvious thing—about legal services is that you don't always need lawyers. These rights that are out there are rights that folks who don't have a law degree can enforce. The gung-ho, aggressive advocates out here before me probably number a great many more than there are in any law school any place in this country. So I would urge that you don't always need a lawyer to bring your 504 complaint, to bring your 503 complaint, or even, for that matter, to bring a lawsuit, which in a federal court just requires 15 bucks and filing a piece of paper—which is called a complaint—stating that your rights have been violated.

But let me urge you that in litigation in particular, and even in 503 and 504 complaints, it may be of some value to get the advice of a lawyer or to retain a lawyer to bring a lawsuit. In that regard, let me suggest that one of the great untapped sources of legal help is the legal services movement, the legal services community of which I am a part. Right now there are over 10,000 full-time, salaried legal services lawyers who are free to low- and moderate-income people throughout the country, and who are available in most areas of the country to provide free legal services. There should be one in your area or your community, and perhaps a number of you have already tagged base with that local office.

Those offices are harried; they do have heavy caseloads; and like any other agency that you've had dealings with, you may have to take an aggressive stance with them, to demand that you be included in their service offering. They are offices that can provide advice, representation to individuals, law reform work (that is, if you're working on legislation in your particular state or on federal legislation, they could be of some assistance in drafting laws or in doing some lobbying with you). They can participate in test case litigation to open up doors that have been totally closed before. They can also provide organizational help to a local organization—advice on incorporating, or advice of a legal nature, or any kind that an organization needs. . . .

I would suggest, if you haven't tagged base with your local legal services or legal aid office—the name varies in different communities—you might want to sit down with the local director and explain the needs of your organization or your community to that person and see what type of offering could be made. Perhaps an individual lawyer can be assigned to take responsibility to be accountable to your local group.

The issues on which legal services lawyers have done a fair bit of tough litigating and aggressive lawyering have been not only in the civil rights area that I've been talking about, but also in the area of SSI and Social Security. Right now there are a number of lawsuits: We've been working with and representing Ted Young's group in Philadelphia and Pennsylvania to sue the Social Security Administration for their failure to observe past income disregards for blind people in Pennsylvania. [These are disregards] that the Social Security Administration—in run-

ning the SSI system—has either intentionally or negligently (we think intentionally) failed to include in the SSI system.

There are some dynamite welfare rights lawyers in the legal services movement who are knowledgeable about SSI and Social Security law, and I would urge you to take advantage of them in whatever local community you live. They are also available to deal with housing problems, consumer issues, a host of family law problems; and they are there to be taken advantage of.

If you are also looking elsewhere, large law firms which are doing well monetarily and have a large staff of lawyers are sometimes available to do what is called "pro bono" (or public interest), free legal work. That can be kind of an iffy thing, and maybe it's more "if" and unavailable than available, but view it as an access, . . . where you want to get to the right people, you want to make your voice heard, and get access to lawyers who often can be made available if they are simply informed that there is a legal need around.

One bonus for the private bar—and this is a new development for private attorneys, and really for all attorneys— To the extent that one is bringing a civil rights lawsuit now, under a civil rights act—and these are mainly the older civil rights acts which cover any suit against a state or local agency, but not yet under 504 unless 504 is against a state or local agency—there is a Civil Rights Attorneys Fee Act of 1976, which is an incentive to private lawyers to get a fee from the opposing party in a case where [the private lawyer] prevails. That's a new development to encourage lawyers to take civil rights lawsuits.

Let me say in conclusion that laws, whether they be in statutes or in court decisions, are only as good or as meaningful as people will make them. And laws need people who are organized to ensure that they will really benefit people. Let me urge you in that regard to stay organized, to stay strong, and to keep your voices clear and loud.

INDEX

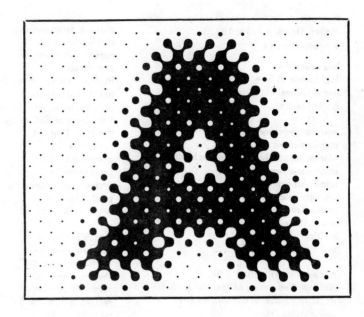

STAFF

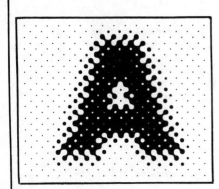

Publisher | John Quirk

Director of Design | Donald Burns

Staff Consultant | Dona Chiappe

Appendix: Agencies and Services for Exceptional Children

Alexander Graham Bell Association for the Deaf,
Inc.
Volta Bureau for the Deaf
3417 Volta Place, NW
Washington, D.C. 20007

American Academy of Pediatrics
1801 Hinman Avenue
Evanston, Illinois 60204

American Association for Gifted Children
15 Gramercy Park
New York, N.Y. 10003

American Association on Mental Deficiency
5201 Connecticut Avenue, NW
Washington, D.C. 20015

American Association of Psychiatric Clinics for
Children
250 West 57th Street
New York, N.Y.

American Bar Association
Commission on the Mentally Disabled
1800 M Street, NW
Washington, D.C. 20036

American Foundation for the Blind
15 W. 16th Street
New York, N.Y. 10011

American Medical Association
535 N. Dearborn Street
Chicago, Illinois 60610

American Speech and Hearing Association
9030 Old Georgetown Road
Washington, D.C. 20014

Association for the Aid of Crippled Children
345 E. 46th Street
New York, N.Y. 10017

Association for Children with Learning Disabilities
2200 Brownsville Road
Pittsburgh, Pennsylvania 15210

Association for Education of the Visually
Handicapped
1604 Spruce Street
Philadelphia, Pennsylvania 19103

Association for the Help of Retarded Children
200 Park Avenue, South
New York, N.Y.

Association for the Visually Handicapped
1839 Frankfort Avenue
Louisville, Kentucky 40206

Center on Human Policy
Division of Special Education and Rehabilitation
Syracuse University
Syracuse, New York 13210

Child Fund
275 Windsor Street
Hartford, Connecticut 06120

Children's Defense Fund
1520 New Hampshire Avenue NW
Washington, D.C. 20036

Closer Look
National Information Center for the Handicapped
1201 Sixteenth Street NW
Washington, D.C. 20036

Clifford W. Beers Guidance Clinic
432 Temple Street
New Haven, Connecticut 06510

Child Study Center
Yale University
333 Cedar Street
New Haven, Connecticut 06520

Child Welfare League of America, Inc.
44 East 23rd Street
New York, N.Y. 10010

Children's Bureau
United States Department of Health, Education
and Welfare
Washington, D.C.

Council for Exceptional Children
1411 Jefferson Davis Highway
Arlington, Virginia 22202

Epilepsy Foundation of America
1828 "L" Street NW
Washington, D.C. 20036

Gifted Child Society, Inc.
59 Glen Gray Road
Oakland, New Jersey 07436

Institute for the Study of Mental Retardation
and Related Disabilities
130 South First
University of Michigan
Ann Arbor, Michigan 48108

International Association for the Scientific Study
of Mental Deficiency
Ellen Horn, AAMD
5201 Connecticut Avenue NW
Washington, D.C. 20015

International League of Societies for the Mentally
Handicapped
Rue Forestiere 12
Brussels, Belgium

Joseph P. Kennedy, Jr. Foundation
1701 K Street NW
Washington, D.C. 20006

League for Emotionally Disturbed Children
171 Madison Avenue
New York, N.Y.

Muscular Dystrophy Associations of America
1790 Broadway
New York, N.Y. 10019

National Aid to the Visually Handicapped
3201 Balboa Street
San Francisco, California 94121

National Association of Coordinators of State
Programs for the Mentally Retarded
2001 Jefferson Davis Highway
Arlington, Virginai 22202

National Association of Hearing and Speech
Agencies
919 18th Street NW
Washington, D.C. 20006

National Association for Creative Children and
Adults
8080 Springvalley Drive
Cincinnati, Ohio 45236
(Mrs. Ann F. Isaacs, Executive Director)

National Association for Retarded Children
420 Lexington Avenue
New York, N.Y.

National Association for Retarded Citizens
2709 Avenue E East
Arlington, Texas 76010

National Children's Rehabilitation Center
P.O. Box 1260
Leesburg, Virginia

National Association for the Visually Handicapped
3201 Balboa Street
San Francisco, California 94121

National Association of the Deaf
814 Thayer Avenue
Silver Spring, Maryland 20910

National Cystic Fibrosis Foundation
3379 Peachtree Road NE
Atlanta, Georgia 30326

National Easter Seal Society for Crippled Children
and Adults
2023 W. Ogden Avenue
Chicago, Illinois 60612

National Federation of the Blind
218 Randolph Hotel
Des Moines, Iowa 50309

National Paraplegia Foundation
333 N. Michigan Avenue
Chicago, Illinois 60601

National Society for Autistic Children
621 Central Avenue
Albany, N.Y. 12206

National Society for Prevention of Blindness, Inc.
79 Madison Avenue
New York, N.Y. 10016

Orton Society, Inc.
8415 Bellona Lane
Baltimore, Maryland 21204

President's Committee on Mental Retardation
Regional Office Building #3
7th and D Streets SW
Room 2614
Washington, D.C. 20201

United Cerebral Palsy Associations
66 E 34th Street
New York, N.Y. 10016

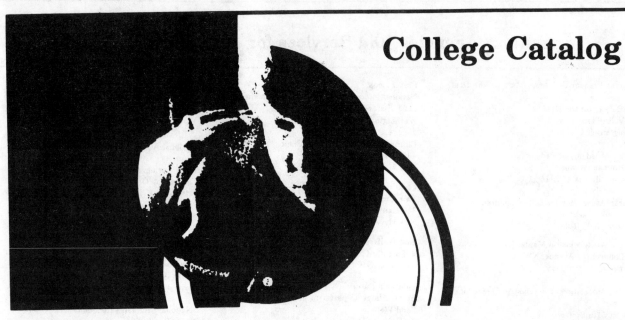

College Catalog

SPECIAL LEARNING CORPORATION

The Special Learning Corporation has developed a series of readers designed for the college student in preparation for teaching exceptional children. Each reader in this high quality series closely follows a college course of study in the special education field. Sending for our free college catalog will provide you with a complete listing of this series, along with a selection of instructional materials and media appropriate for use in special education.

For further information
please contact:

College Catalog Division
Special Learning Corporation

SPECIAL LEARNING CORPORATION
42 Boston Post Rd. Guilford, Conn. 06437